Bordeaux
Wines, Wineries, Tasting & Travel

Jacques Racon

Table of Contents

Welcome to the Bordeaux Wine Region!

World famous wine varietals are produced in the Bordeaux region of southwestern France. With centuries of tradition, its distinct vintages erupt from Bordeaux's ideal grape-growing terroirs.

The Bordeaux region is cut in two by the Gironde estuary and there is a marked difference between wines from its Left and Right Banks. The Left Bank is dominated by the "Super Four" wine estates – the appellations of Pauillac, Margaux, Saint Julien and Saint Estephe – where Bordeaux's most prestigious wine chateaux are found.

Graves to the south offers more history with glamorous connections to medieval kings, queens and popes as well as the "happy accident" of noble rot, which lends a seductively sweet character to the golden-hued whites from Sauternes and Barsac.

On the Right Bank – which is located to the north and east of the Dordogne River – you can visit the medieval charm of St Emilion. The picturesque little town at the heart of the appellation of the same name is home to vineyards that go back to Roman times and is the birthplace of "garage wine", the latest controversial trend in Bordeaux. In general, Right Bank vineyards tend to be smaller and more compact and its Merlot dominated vintages are softer on the palate than the tannin rich wines of the Left Bank.

It is impossible to cover each winery in Bordeaux – there are well over 8,000 of them – but an attempt has been made to include as many of the classified growths as possible. The anecdotes, legends and pop culture references of brands such as Lafite Rothschild, Château Latour, Château d'Yquem, Chateau Mouton Rothschild and Petrus add to the intrigue of Bordeaux wines but not all of the top wineries are equally accessible to casual visitors. Tastes also differ and wine lovers may find themselves deriving more pleasure from a well-blended Bourgeois Cru than a Famous First Growth.

A visit to Bordeaux should be less about ticking off tasting bucket lists and more about having a truly individual experience in one of the world's great wine regions.

Bordeaux Wine Classification

The Wine Classification of 1855 is a direct result of the Exposition Universelle, an international trade fair organized by Napoleon III in response to the Great Exhibition at Crystal Palace. This prestigious event drew participants from over 20 different countries and was visited by more than 5 million people. The emperor requested the establishment of a wine classification table from the Bordeaux Chamber of Commerce, who in turn delegated the job to the Syndicat of Courtiers, an association of wine brokers.

The original classification lists 4 Premier Crus (First Growths), 14 Deuxièmes Crus (Second Growths), 14 Troisièmes Crus (Third Growths), 10 Quatrièmes Crus (Fourth Growths) and 18 Cinqièmes Crus (Fifth Growths).

The Original 1855 List

Premier Grand Crus/First Growths

Château Lafite Rothschild, Pauillac
Château Latour, Pauillac
Château Margaux, Margaux
Château Haut-Brion Pessac, Graves (renamed to Pessac-Leognan in 1986)

Deuxiemes Crus/Second Growths

Château Mouton-Rothschild (a first-growth since 1973) Pauillac
Château Rausan-Segla Margaux
Château Rauzan-Gassies Margaux
Château Léoville Las Cases St.-Julien
Château Léoville Poyferré St.-Julien
Château Léoville Barton St.-Julien
Château Durfort-Vivens Margaux
Château Gruaud-Larose St.-Julien
Château Lascombes (Margaux - original name Domaine de Lascombes)
Château Brane-Cantenac (Margaux)
Château Pichon-Longueville-Baron Pauillac
Château Pichon Longueville Comtesse de Lalande (Pichon-Longueville-Lalande) Pauillac
Château Ducru-Beaucaillou St.-Julien
Château Cos-d'Estournel St.-Estèphe
Château Montrose St.-Estèphe

Troisièmes Crus/Third Growths

Château Kirwan Cantenac-Margaux (Margaux)
Château d'Issan Cantenac-Margaux (Margaux)
Château Lagrange St.-Julien
Château Langoa Barton St.-Julien
Château Giscours (Margaux)
Château Malescot-St.-Exupéry Margaux
Château Cantenac-Brown Cantenac-Margaux (Margaux)
Château Boyd-Cantenac Margaux
Château Palmer Cantenac-Margaux (Margaux)
Château La Lagune Ludon (Haut-Médoc)
Château Desmirail Margaux
Château Calon-Ségur St.-Estephe
Château Ferrière Margaux
Château Marquis-d'Alesme-Becker Margaux

Quatrièmes Crus/Fourth Growths

Château St.-Pierre St.-Julien
Château Talbot St.-Julien
Château Branaire-Ducru St.-Julien
Château Duhart-Milon Rothschild Pauillac
Château Pouget Cantenac (Margaux)
Château La Tour Carnet St.-Laurent (Haut-Médoc)
Château Lafon-Rochet St.-Estèphe
Château Beychevelle St.-Julien
Château Prieuré-Lichine Cantenac-Margaux (Margaux)
Château Marquis de Terme Margaux

Cinqièmes Crus/Fifth Growths

Château Pontet-Canet Pauillac
Château Batailley Pauillac
Château Haut-Batailley Pauillac
Château Grand-Puy-Lacoste Pauillac
Château Grand-Puy-Ducasse Pauillac
Château Lynch-Bages Pauillac
Château Lynch-Moussas Pauillac
Château Dauzac Labarde (Margaux)
Château Mouton-Baronne-Philippe (Château d'Armailhac after 1989) Pauillac
Château du Tertre Arsac (Margaux)
Château Haut-Bages-Libéral Pauillac
Château Pédesclaux Pauillac
Château Belgrave St.-Laurent (Haut-Médoc)
Château Camensac (Château de Camensac) St.-Laurent (Haut-Médoc)
Château Cos-Labory St.-Estèphe
Château Clerc-Milon Pauillac
Château Croizet-Bages Pauillac
Château Cantemerle (Haut-Médoc)

Amendments

Château Cantemerle (Haut-Médoc) was added to the Fifth Growths in 1856. This winery was meant to be included in the 1855 Classification but was left off the Bordeaux map at the Exposition due to an administrative error.

In 1973, Château Mouton-Rothschild was elevated to the prestigious First Growth classification.

Sauternes Classification

The Sauternes Classification is for sweet white wine and was also originally determined in 1855. There are two basic classes, Premiers crus (first growths) and Deuxiemes Crus (second growths), with one wine outranking all by being awarded superior first growth status.

Premier cru supérieur

Chateau d'Yquem (Sauternes)

Premiers crus

Chateau Climens (Barsac)
Chateau Clos Haut Peyraguey (Bommes)
Chateau Coutet (Barsac)
Chateau Guiraud (Sauternes)
Chateau Lafaurie Peyraguey (Bommes)
Chateau Rabaud Promis (Bommes)
Chateau Rayne Vigneau (Bommes)
Chateau Rieussec (Fargues)
Chateau Sigalas Rabaud (Bommes)
Chateau Suduiraut (Preignac)
Chateau La Tour Blanche (Bommes)

Seconds crus

Chateau d'Arche (Sauternes)
Chateau Broustet (Barsac)
Chateau Caillou (Barsac)
Chateau Doisy Daëne (Barsac)
Chateai Doisy Dubroca (Barsac)
Chateau Doisy Védrines (Barsac)
Chateau Filhot (Sauternes)
Chateau Lamothe Guignard (Sauternes)
Chateau de Malle (Preignac)
Chateau Myrat (Barsac)
Chateau Nairac (Barsac)
Chateau Romer-du Hayot (Fargues)

Graves Classification

With the exception of Chateau Haute Brion, no wines from the Graves appellation were considered for the Classification of 1855. Almost a century later, the same criteria were used for determining the Graves classes. An unofficial list was generated in 1953 and this was formalized in 1959, classification for the appellation of Graves was formalized. The estates that were awarded Grand Cru status are:

Chateau Bouscaut (red and white)
Chateau Carbonnieux (red and white)
Chateau Couhins (white)
Chateau Couhins Lurton (white)
Chateau Fieuzal (red)
Chateau Haut-Bailly (red)
Chatau Haut-Brion (red)
Chateau La Mission Haut-Brion (red)
Chateau Latour Haut-Brion (red)

Chateau Latour Martillac (red and white)
Chateau Laville Haut-Brion (white)
Chateau Malartic Lagravière (red and white)
Chateau Olivier (red and white)
Chateau Pape Clément (red)
Chateau Smith Haut-Lafitte (red)
Domaine de Chevalier (red and white)

St Emilion Classification (2012)

The wines from St Emilion were first classified in 1955, with the intention to update the list on a 10 yearly basis. It was updated in 1969, 1986, 1996 and most recently 2012. Controversy surrounds the 1996 list and in 2012 the classification was outsourced.

Premiers Grands Crus Classés (A)

Chateau Angelus
Chateau Ausone
Chateau Cheval Blanc
Chateau Pavie

Premiers Grands Crus Classés (B)

Chateau Beausejour
Chateau Beausejour Becot
Chateau Belair Monange
Chateau Canon
Château Canon-la-Gaffelière
Château Figeac
Clos Fourtet
Château La Gaffelière
Château Larcis-Ducasse
Château La Mondotte
Château Pavie-Macquin
Château Troplong Mondot
Château Trotte Vieille
Château Valandraud

Grands crus classés

Château l'Arrosée, Château Balestard-la Tonnelle, Château Barde-Haut, Château Bellefont-Belcier, Château Bellevue, Château Berliquet, Château Cadet Bon, Château Cap de Mourlin, Château Chauvin, Château le Chatelet, Château Clos de Sarpe, Château la Clotte, Château la Commanderie, Château Corbin, Château Côte de Baleau, Château la Couspaude, Château Dassault, Château Destieux, Château la Dominique, Château Faugères, Château Faurie de Souchard, Château de Ferrand, Château Fleur-Cardinale, Château La Fleur Morange, Château Fombrauge, Château Fonplégade, Château Fonroque, Château Franc Mayne,

Château Grand Corbin, Château Grand Corbin-Despagne, Château Grand Mayne, Château les Grandes Murailles, Château Grand Pontet, Château Guadet, Château Haut Sarpe, Clos des Jacobins, Couvent des Jacobins, Château Jean Faure, Château Laniote, Château Larmande, Château Laroque, Château Laroze, Château la Madelaine, Château La Marzelle, Château Monbousquet, Château Moulin du Cadet, Clos de l'Oratoire, Château Pavie-Decesse, Château Peby Faugères, Château Petit Faurie de Soutard, Château de Pressac, Château Le Prieuré, Château Quinault l'Enclos, Château Ripeau, Château Rochebelle, Château Saint Georges-Côte Pavie, Clos Saint-Martin, Château Sansonnet, Château La Serre, Château Soutard, Château Tertre Daugay, Château La Tour Figeac, Château Villemaurine, Château Yon Figeac.

Cru Bourgeois Classification

From 1932, the Bordeaux Chamber of Commerce and Chamber of Agriculture have drawn up a list of Cru Bourgeois. This defines wine chateaux that fall below the 1855 classification but produce wines of quality. In 2003, a three-tier subdivision was introduced to Cru Bourgeois wines, but this was banned from 2007 and in 2010, a single level Cru Bourgeois classification was reinstated. The lists are traditionally published two years after the vintages included in it. Any winery from the Médoc region can apply to have their wines evaluated for inclusion. Participation is voluntary.

The most recent lists of selection can be accessed at the following link (http://www.crus-bourgeois.com/spip.php?article55#spip.php?article54&lang=en) , while the original 1932 list is available here (http://www.crus-bourgeois.com/IMG/UserFiles/Files/Liste_Crus_Bourgeois_Medoc_1932.pdf).

The three tiers of the 2003 ranking were Exceptionnel, Supérieurs and Bourgeois. After the restructuring of 2010, 6 of the 9 wineries that occupied the top tier elected for exclusion and instead adopted the Les Exceptionnels label to brand their vintages. These wineries are Château Chasse-Spleen (Moulis-en-Médoc), Château Les Ormes-de-Pez (Saint-Estèphe), Château de Pez (Saint-Estèphe), Château Potensac (Médoc), Château Poujeaux (Moulis-en-Médoc) and Château Siran (Margaux).

In 2006, the Cru Artisan classification was reintroduced, after it had fallen in disuse in the 1930s. Cru Artisan defines family estates that grow, produce and market their own wines. It is restricted to 44 estates, but will be revised on a 10-yearly basis. Cru Artisan is ranked just below Cru Bourgeois.

Grape Types

Ten grape varieties can be marketed with the Bordeaux name. Wines containing other grape types do not qualify to be marketed as Bordeaux wines and must instead bear the more generic label of Vin de France (French wine).

There are six red and four white varieties from Bordeaux. They are Cabernet Sauvignon (red), Merlot (red), Cabernet Franc (red), Petit Verdot (red), Malbec (red) Carmenere (red), Sauvignon Blanc (white), Semillon (white), Muscadelle (white) and Sauvignon Gris (white).

Cabernet Sauvignon

Cabernet Sauvignon is one of the most common grapes in the Bordeaux region. The grape resulted from the pairing of Cabernet Franc and Sauvignon Blanc grapes in the 17th century. Because they are so hardy and durable, Cabernet Sauvignon grapes are planted in a wide variety of regions, including Canada, California, New Zealand, Lebanon and South Africa, but they first rose to prominence in the Bordeaux region. The grapes are thick-skinned and rich in tannin, resulting in dry, full-bodied wines that mature quite well. The wine has a dark hue and is characterized by an aroma of blackcurrant and cedar wood. Typically, the alcohol content settles around 13.5 percent, although it may go as high as 15 percent. Given the strong taste, Cabernet Sauvignon wines can be enjoyed with hearty foods such as steak.

Merlot

Merlot produces a versatile grape variety that is great for blending with other grapes. It ripens quicker than Cabernet but its thin skin makes it more susceptible to adverse environmental factors such as rot and frost. There is a difference in aroma between cool climate and warm climate Merlots. Bordeaux's Merlot is typical of a cool climate Merlot with an alcohol content of around 13.5 percent and an aroma of plum, with an undertone of tobacco and tar. It is low in tannin levels.

Merlot has been historically identified as a pairing of Cabernet Franc and a rare grape known as Magdeleine Noire de Charentes.

With its soft, fruity taste, Merlot is easy on the palate making it a good entry level red wine to introduce those new to wine tasting. It can be enjoyed with food or on its own. Merlot is currently the most planted grape variety in Bordeaux and, together with Cabernet Sauvignon, is a cornerstone of many Bordeaux wines.

Cabernet Franc

Cabernet Franc is a black grape variety that compliments a variety of food types with its slightly spicy aroma. It first rose to prominence in the Loire Valley in the 1600s and from the 1700s it became a mainstay of Bordeaux wines. As the third most popular grape type in Bordeaux, it is also a parent grape to several other Bordeaux grape types such as Cabernet Sauvignon, Carménère and Merlot.

Cabernet Franc flourishes in cool climates and ripens about a week earlier than Cabernet Sauvignon. On the right bank, particularly around St Emilion and Pomerol, it is an important blending wine. Dominant aromas are of plum, strawberry and roasted peppers.

Malbec

Malbec is a more rare, purple variety of grape that is descended from the Magdeleine Noire des Charentes. It grew popular during the 1700s and the first half of the 1800s, but since its thin skin makes it sensitive to rot, frost and other ills, it has declined considerably in stature in Bordeaux.

Malbec is also a popular component of Argentine vineyards as it thrives in that country's sunny dry climate.

Malbec is characterized by its plum flavor, robust tannin levels and low acidity. It mixes well with various types of red meat.

Petite Verdot

Petite Verdot is a variety of red grape that produces a bold, full-bodied wine. It is characterized by a floral aroma and carries overtones of plum, blackberry, cherry, violet, lilac lavender and sage. When age in oak, there are also smoky hints of vanilla, hazelnut and mocha. Petite Verdot is rich in color and tannin content. It ripens late and is seldom used as a single component of wine. In Bordeaux, it is mainly a blending wine.

Carménère

Carménère is an ancient grape varietal that occurs in small, isolated tracts of Bordeaux. It is believed to date back to Roman winemaking in France and may have originated in Iberia. In the cool climate of Bordeaux, it is difficult to cultivate to the flowering stage and highly susceptible to coulure (shatter) and mildew. The Phylloxera epidemic made it harder to find in the region after the mid-1800s.

Carménère also thrives in the warmer climate of Chile in South America. It is crimson in color, with a spicy, smoky aroma that combines well with spicy food and strong-flavored cheeses.

Sauvignon Blanc

Sauvignon Blanc is one of the most planted grapes in the world. It is a green variety that produces white wine with the flavor of green apple, lime and green bell pepper. In the cooler climate of Bordeaux, its slow ripening produces a delicate balance between the sugar and acidity of the wine. It is often used as a blending wine.

Sémillon

Sémillon is a thin-skinned white grape variety that is fairly easy to grow, but prone to rot. During the 18th and 19th century, it was one of the most common grape types in New World vineyards, particularly in South Africa, Australia and Chile.

In Bordeaux, Sémillon dominates in the appellations of Sauternes and Barsac where the propensity of Botrytis cinerea infection results in a distinctively sweet wine.

Sémillon is often blended with Sauvignon Blanc and Muscadelle. In Graves and Pessac-Léognan, it is used for dry whites.

Sauvignon Gris

Sauvignon Gris is a rare grape type that resulted from a mutation of Sauvignon Blanc. In Bordeaux, Sauvignon Gris represents only 2 percent of the vineyards of the region. Although the skin is pinkish in hue, the fruit inside is white and it produces a white wine. Sauvignon Gris is high in sugar and produces a dry, herbaceous wine with undertones of mango, melon and citrus.

In Bordeaux, unblended Sauvignon Gris must be labelled as generic white Bordeaux. In Bordeaux, Sauvignon Gris is often harvested early in the season.

Muscadelle

Muscadelle is a white grape variety that often adds a floral aroma to wines. In Bordeaux, Muscadelle is used in sweet and dry white wines, usually as a minor component blended with Semillon and Sauvignon Blanc. It is also grown in Australia, where it is used to make a fortified white wine known as Topaque.

How to Taste Wine

1. Look at the wine and examine its color. This is best viewed against a white background. The color of a wine is evaluated on a spectrum ranging from translucent to dense. Thirty-six distinct wine hues have been identified by wine experts and these can indicate a number of characteristics of your wine. For example, a brown hue can indicate oxidization or aging. A golden tinge is also associated with aging, particularly in white wines. Additionally, the wine's acidity can be indicated by its color. Wines with a high acidity level will be vividly red, while wines with a bluish tinge will express lower acidity levels. A lining of magenta may reveal the presence of Malbec grapes. You should also be able to see whether the wine is clear or carries some sediment. Sediment is more commonly found in red wines that have already aged a bit.

2. Swirl the wine in the glass by making gentle, circular movements. This is done to increase or amplify its smell, but can also reveal its consistency, weight and texture. Wines with a substantial weight and texture are commonly referred to as full-bodied. Swirling will provide a few hints about the wine's alcohol content, by revealing the "legs" (or tears) of the wine. The term "legs" refers to the rate at which a wine evaporates from the glass and wines with higher alcohol content will have thicker legs that move a little slower.

3. Smell the Wine. This will reveal the fruit in a wine's aromas. You may also detect aromas of herbs, spice, mineral or different types of earth, when examining its olfactory qualities. You should be able to detect an aroma of oak, if oak barrels were used in the aging process, but this may also unlock scents of cedar, vanilla, spice, chocolate and cigar. Aromas result from the combination of grape type, fermentation and aging.

4. Taste the wine. Swish it around your mouth to spread the wine around the different taste centers and hold it in your mouth for a few seconds. You will detect any noticeable sweetness at the tip of your tongue. This will be absent in a dry wine. Sweetness is what adds calories to a wine, although strong tannins or acidity may mask the residual sugars in certain wines. Acidity will reveal itself through a tingling sensation on your tongue and this may be strong or medium. Highly acidic wines will taste tart, while wines with a lower acidity level will seem creamier or even flat. Tannins make wine taste dry when present and this is best detected from the tip to the center of the tongue. Alcohol often reveals the intensity of a wine. This also plays a role in the body or texture of a wine.

Food Pairings

Good food and wine pairing has the potential to increase the taste sensation enjoyed when drinking a specific wine. Some tastes and flavors mingle and complement better than others. There are certain basic guidelines but you should enjoy experimenting to find your own pairing preferences.

When serving meat, the color of the wine should match that of the meat. Red wines typically combine well with red meats such as beef, lamb and venison. Darker fowl such as guinea fowl and ostrich can also be matched with a red wine.

White wine is good for accompanying white meats like turkey and chicken and also fish.

Certain cuts go better with certain types of wine. Lean beef cuts, venison and lamb will be well-matched with a medium bodied wine, while the fattier cuts go better with full-bodied reds that carry a higher alcohol content.

Tomato based sauces call for wine with a fairly high acidity level. Brown sauces like Bordelaise and Demi-Glace go well with bold, earthy reds. Fruity red wines can be matched with green sauces such as mint or tangy sauces such as BBQ and Hoisin.

Chocolate and dessert go well with sweet wines from Sauternes and we suggest the wine should be a little sweeter than its companion food. Dark chocolate with a strong cocoa content (between 60 and 85 percent) is good for pairing with red wine.

Other good matches with sweet dessert wines are sushi, foie gras, creamy cheeses, cheesecake and fruit tart.

Combine salads with fairly acidic wines. Earthy wines complement mushrooms. Rich meaty dishes will find their match in powerfully tannic red wines.

Left Bank Appellations

The Left Bank of Bordeaux is divided into two sub-regions. The area north of the city of Bordeaux is the Medoc. To the south is Graves.

Medoc

Although the Medoc comprises the entire region north of the city Bordeaux, the Medoc label also applies to wines not defined by any of the other appellations that fall within the region.

Pauillac

Pauillac is located along the left bank of the Gironde Estuary, between the river and Canal du Midi, north of the city of Bordeaux. The town has a few interesting 19th century structures and a nearby marina which berths 155 vessels. Nearby is the picturesque hamlet of Bages, with numerous quaint shops and cafes.

Pauillac is home to 115 vine growers, among them 18 classified crus and three that occupy the top tier of First Growth, namely Chateau Latour, Château Lafite Rothschild and Chateau Mouton Rothschild, making its name a mark of class and distinction. The appellation typically produces a tannic, full-bodied red with aromas of blackcurrant, dark berry and cedar.

The **Chateau Latour** (http://www.chateau-latour.com/) wine estate is located at the southern end of Pauillac, bordering the vineyards of Chateau Léoville Las Cases in Saint Julien. It is one of the oldest wineries in the area. Its name is derived from the Saint-Lambert tower, a fortified structure from the Hundred Year War that used to stand on the property.

The estate dates back at least to the 14th century and from the 18th century was connected with the de Ségur family who also once owned Lafite Rothschild and Mouton Rothschild.

At the time of Thomas Jefferson's French residency as French ambassador for the United States of America, Chateau Latour was considered one of the top wines by the French aristocracy and in 1855, it was one of only four wines to be granted the coveted First Growth classification.

Chateau Latour grows 74 percent Cabernet Sauvignon, 23 percent Merlot, as well as a small portion of Cabernet Franc and Petit Verdot.

Some of its vines are close to a century old and specific tracts of land are dedicated to the production of its Grand Vin and its second wine, Les Forts de Latour, affording each their own character. Chateau Latour is described as a full-bodied, tannic wine with tones of spice, truffles and tobacco. A third wine, Pauillac de Latour, is produced from the younger vines. Tours can be arranged by appointment only, via a contact form on the website.

Although **Château Lafite Rothschild** (http://www.lafite.com/) is located in the Pauillac appellation, it also uses a few hectares of vineyard in Saint Estèphe. Ownership of the property can be traced back to Gombaud de Lafite, a 13th century abbot of the Vertheuil Monastery, but most of its vineyards were planted in the 17th century under Jacques de Ségur. In the early 18th century, Marquis Nicolas Alexandre de Ségur perfected the vintage, gaining the moniker of "The Wine Prince". His wine became celebrated at Versailles, where it was known as 'the king's wine' and 'ambrosia of the Gods of Olympus'. Thomas Jefferson described it as one of the four finest wines of Bordeaux. It was hardly surprising that Château Lafite Rothschild was awarded the coveted First Growth status at the 1855 Classification. Baron James Mayer Rothschild bought the property in 1868 and currently, it is managed by Baron Eric de Rothschild, fifth generation of the Rothschild family.

Château Lafite Rothschild is one of the largest vineyards in the Medoc. It grows 70 percent Cabernet Sauvignon, 25 percent Merlot, 3 percent Cabernet Franc and 2 percent Petit Verdot. Besides the Grand Vin, there is a second wine, Carruades de Lafite. Château Lafite Rothschild can be visited for guided tours by appointment, for parties no larger than 15 persons. There is an opportunity for wine tasting after the tour.

For many years, **Chateau Mouton Rothschild** (http://www.chateau-mouton-rothschild.com/) was once best known for what it was not. With the 1855 classification of Bordeaux wines, it was the one glaring omission.

Although belonging to the same price group as the other First Growth wines, Château Mouton Rothschild had been grouped with the Second Growths.

In 1973, it was finally elevated to become the fifth of the Premier Crus. The estate was acquired in 1853 from Nicolas-Alexandre de Ségur by Baron Nathaniel de Rothschild, but it truly came into its own from the 1920s, when his great grandson Baron Philippe de Rothschild took over and introduced a number of bold innovations.

Château Mouton Rothschild grows 81 percent Cabernet Sauvignon, 15 percent, Merlot, 3 percent Cabernet Franc and 1 percent Petit Verdot. Its terroir is gravel, with a fairly high vine density. Grapes are picked by hand. They are fermented and matured in casks of oak. Since 1923, the wine has been bottled on site. As a wine, Château Mouton Rothschild is exotic and spicy.

Le Petit Mouton de Mouton Rothschild is the second wine produced on the estate. Its 1970 vintage took second place in the Judgement of Paris competition of 1976. A jeroboam of the 1945 vintage sold for $114,614 when auctioned at Christie's in 1997.

The wine bottles from Château Mouton Rothschild are collectible and the labels are prized. Since 1945, contemporary modern artists have been commissioned to design a unique label for each year. Artists have included Salvador Dali, Andy Warhol, Joan Miro, Francis Bacon, Georges Braque and Henry Moore. The 1973 label was dedicated to Pablo Picasso, who died that year. In 1977, Rothschild labels celebrated a visit to the Chateau by the Queen Mother. Labels for 1953 and 2003 marked the 100 and 150th anniversary of Baron Nathaniel de Rothschild's acquisition of the estate.

Chateau Mouton Rothschild is open to the public by prior appointment. One of its attractions is the Museum of Wine in Art with a splendid collection of tapestries, paintings, gold, silverware, glassware and porcelain. The original artwork for the wine labels is exhibited in a gallery next to the vat room. To visit, fill in the reservation form on the website.

Château Pichon Comtesse and Château Pichon Longueville Baron were once part of the larger estate created by Pierre de Rauzan, a 17th century wine merchant and former manager at Château Latour. Located at the southern end of Pauillac, near the St Julian border, the estates were split in 1850 when Baron Joseph de Pichon Longueville died, leaving his estate to his five children. The estate of the two sons became Château Pichon Longueville Baron and the estate of his three daughters became Château Pichon Longueville Comtesse de Lalande. Each of the estates evolved to produce a distinct wine, both excellent enough to be awarded Second Growth status with the 1855 Classification. Pierre de Rauzan is also associated with two Second Growth estates from the Margaux appellation, namely Château Rauzan-Ségla and Château Rauzan-Gassies.

Château Pichon Baron (http://www.pichonbaron.com/en/) remained in the de Pichon Longueville family until 1933. After a period of decline, it made a powerful comeback to its former excellence in the 1990s. Pichon Baron grows 70 percent Cabernet Sauvignon, 25 percent Merlot, 3 percent Cabernet Franc and 2 percent Petit Verdot. The Grand Vin is rich, spicy, full-bodied and tannic. It is at its best after at least 10 years in the cellar. A second wine, Les Tourelles de Longueville, was introduced in 1986.

The estate shares a connection with **Château Pibran**, a small estate that sends its grapes to Château Pichon Baron for vinification and currently carries Cru Bourgeois classification. Through its current manager, Christian Seely, it is also linked to Chateau Suduiraut in Sauternes and Chateau Petit Village in Pomerol. Château Pichon Baron is open to the public by appointment on weekdays and weekends. Tours cost €15/person and are available in English, French, German, Spanish and Chinese.

Château Pichon Longueville Comtesse de Lalande
(http://www.pichon-lalande.com/) had a long tradition of
female leadership from Countess de Lalande to May-
Eliane de Lencquesaing. Current ownership is under
Frederic Rouzaud who is also connected with Chateau
Bernadotte, Chateau de Pez, Haut Beausejour and
Chateau Reaut la Graviere. The estate grows 45 percent
Cabernet Sauvignon, 35 percent Merlot, 12 percent
Cabernet Franc and 8 percent Petit Verdot. It produces a
sensuous, exotic wine, which is somewhat less tannic
than that of Château Pichon Baron. The wine is best after
ten years of aging.

Château Duhart-Milon Rothschild
(http://www.lafite.com/en/the-chateaus/chateau-duhart-milon/)
borders Lafite Rothschild. Sir Duhart was said to be a
pirate in the service of Louis XV, who settled in the Médoc
for retirement. A "pirate's house", which used to be on the
property, is remembered on the wine's label. This Fourth
Growth estate was purchased by the Rothschild family in
1962 and it now is under Lafite Rothschild.

Château Batailley (http://www.batailley.com/en.html) can
be found on a plateau to the west of Mouton Rothschild. It
is one of the older estates in the area, taking its name
from a battle of the Hundred Year War that took place
here in the 15th century.

Château Batailley's wine had been termed a Fifth Growth
as far back as 1815 and the 1855 Classification made it
official. The property was purchased in 1932 by two
brothers, François and Marcel Borie, who subdivided it in
1942. The larger property remained Château Batailley
while a smaller segment became the **Château Haut-
Batailley** (http://www.chateau-haut-batailley.com/en/).

Two Fifth Growth estates can be found on Grand Puy, a low gravelly hill in the Pauillac appellation. Once part of the same estate, they were split when a portion of the vineyards were sold to Pierre Ducasse in 1750 to become **Château Grand-Puy-Ducasse** (http://www.grandpuyducasse.fr/en/). Its Grand du Vin is a blend of Cabernet Sauvignon and Merlot. It has a complex aroma and is drinkable after five years but has the potential to age to 20-25 years.

The remainder of the original estate is now the **Château Grand-Puy-Lacoste** (http://www.chateau-grand-puy-lacoste.com/en/). The present château was built in 1855 when it was classified a Fifth Growth. Château Grand-Puy-Lacoste is now owned by the Borie family who are also associated with Chateau Haut Batailley. The estate grows Cabernet Sauvignon, Merlot and Cabernet Franc. It produces a balanced claret that is at its best between 12 and 30 years as well as a second wine, Lacoste-Borie, which is approachable at an earlier age. The Grand du Vin has aromas of blackcurrant, cassis fruit and cigar box perfume. The estate is also known for its beautiful gardens.

Château Pontet-Canet (http://www.pontet-canet.com/en/) is located at the northern end of Pauillac near Château Mouton Rothschild. It was founded when Jean-François de Pontet, a former Master of the Horse at Versailles and governor of Medoc began to purchase land for a vineyard around 1705. The resulting wine was awarded Fifth Growth status in 1855. In its long history, the estate changed hands twice. It was bought by wine merchant Herman Cruse in 1865. In 1975 the château came into the possession of cognac merchant Guy Tesseron. The current management team is committed to biodynamic farming practices. Draft horses have replaced tractors and harvesting is done by hand. This paid off by producing an intense, full-bodied wine.

Besides the Grand du Vin, Château Pontet-Canet produces a second wine, Les Hauts de Pontet. It maintains one of the largest production operations of a classified growth in Medoc. When visiting you can tour the vineyards, view the vat room and finish off the experience with a taste of the estate's grand cru. Visits are by appointment only.

Chateau Clerc Milon (http://www.chateau-clerc-milon.com/) is a small wine estate located at the northern end of the Pauillac appellation. It borders the prestigious Château Mouton Rothschild and Château Lafite Rothschild. Over the years, it changed hands numerous times. Its wines achieved Fifth Growth status with the 1855 Classification, while under the ownership of Jean-Baptiste Clerc. In 1970, it was acquired by Baron Philippe de Rothschild, owner of Château Mouton Rothschild who set about transforming its image.

Chateau Clerc Milon grows 50 percent Cabernet Sauvignon, 36 percent Merlot, 11 percent Cabernet Franc, 2 percent Petit Verdot and 1 percent Carménère. Most vines at the Chateau are around 53 years old, making it the oldest in the appellation.

Besides Chateau Clerc Milon, a second wine Pastourelle de Clerc Milon was recently introduced. The current administrators of Château Mouton Rothschild have also owned **Château d'Armailhac** (http://www.chateau-darmailhac.com/), another Fifth Growth in Pauillac that was previously known as Château Mouton-Baron Philippe, from the 1930s.

The estate grows 56 percent Cabernet Sauvignon, 22 percent Merlot, 20 percent Cabernet Franc and 2 percent Petit Verdot. It has some of the oldest vines in the Medoc, some going back as far as 1890, but backed up by the research laboratory of Château Mouton Rothschild, it produces a light, elegant wine with a fine concentration of flavors.

Château Pédesclaux (http://www.chateau-pedesclaux.com/) was founded in 1810 by wine broker Pierre Urbain Pédesclaux and awarded Fifth Growth status in 1855. It is now owned by Jacky Lorenzetti who also owns Château Lilian Ladouys in St. Estephe and Chateau d'Issan in Margaux. The grand vin is described as elegant, dense and charming. There is a second wine, Fleur de Pédesclaux which has a Merlot component of around 90 percent.

Château Lynch-Bages (http://www.jmcazes.com/en/chateau-lynch-bages), one of the best-loved estates of Pauillac, is located on a plateau by the little village of Bages. It is named after Thomas Lynch of Irish descent who married Elizabeth Drouillard, its heir. Later, the estate passed into the hands of the Swiss wine merchant, Sebastien Jurine.

From the 1970s the estate fell under the enthusiastic management of Jean-Michel Cazes who modernized its facilities and also increased the estate's profile in the emerging wine tourism region of Bordeaux.

Château Lynch-Bages grows Cabernet Sauvignon, Merlot, Cabernet Franc and Petit Verdot for its reds. There is also a parcel of land dedicated to Sauvignon Blanc, Semillon and Muscadelle. These white wines were first introduced in 1990. Visitors can enjoy a friendly, informative tour and a tasting of the grand vin as well as Echo de Lynch-Bages, its second wine. There is a bakery, brasserie and gift shop.

Château Lynch-Moussas (http://www.lynch-moussas.com/en.html) also was owned by the Lynch family and was acquired early in the 20th century by the Castéja family. From the 1970s its wine-making facilities were upgraded.

Besides the grand vin, a Fifth Growth, Château Lynch-Moussas also produces a second wine, Les Hauts de Lynch-Moussas. **Château Croizet-Bages** has been in a period of decline, but is currently in the process of renovation. **Château Haut-Bages-Libéral** (http://www.hautbagesliberal.com/) produces a wine that is less tannic and softer on the palate than most wines from Pauillac, making it a great choice for an entry level tasting. The estate dates back to the 1700s and is currently managed by Claire Villars-Lurton. Its largest vineyard borders Château Latour.

Margaux

Margaux is the southern-most appellation in the Medoc and it consists of the villages of Margaux, Arsac, Labarde, Soussons and Cantenac. It is home to one famous premier cru or first growth and produces predominantly red wines, which are generally lighter, more approachable and smoother than those of Pauillac.

A little to the north of Margaux lies the picturesque village of Lamarque where a ferry service offers a time-saving connection to Blaye and the Cotes de Blaye wine region.

The land of **Chateau Margaux** (http://www.chateau-margaux.com/en/) has been settled from the 12th century and its association with wine making dates back at least to the 15th century. Originally known as La Mothe de Margaux, the property passed through the hands of several noble families until it came to the possession of Pierre de Lestonnac. He began the process of converting grain lands to vines and by the latter part of the 17th century, the winery at Chateau Margaux was already well-established. It thrived under the visionary administration of a manager known as Berlon. Through his understanding of the soil, he introduced key innovations such as separate vinification for red and white grapes and the practice of harvesting in the latter part of the day. In the 18th century, Chateau Margaux produced the first claret to be listed at Christie's.

The silky, sophisticated grand vin of Chateau Margaux is one of only four wines to achieve First Growth status at the 1855 classification and it was the only wine to achieve a perfect score from the judges. It also won a place in the record books as the most expensive wine ever brokered, when a bottle of Château Margaux 1787 from Thomas Jefferson's celebrated collection was valued at $212,000.

Chateau Margaux produces a second red wine named Pavillon Rouge du Château Margaux, as well as a dry white, Pavillon Blanc du Château Margaux, although the latter does not conform to the appellation's guidelines.

Chateau Margaux grows 75 percent Cabernet Sauvignon, 20 percent Merlot, 3 percent Petit Verdot and 2 percent Cabernet Franc.

In recent years, the estate has adopted 100 percent organic farming methods. A visit to the cellars can be booked by appointment on weekdays only and outside of the harvest period.

Château Durfort-Vivens (http://www.durfort-vivens.fr/en/) was been the property of the Durfort de Duras family for more than 700 years from the 12th century to 1824 when it was purchased by M. de Vivens. The family also owned what was to become Chateau Margaux as well as the estate that later became Château Lascombes.

American wine connoisseur Thomas Jefferson ranked the wines of Château Durfort-Vivens as just below Chateau Lafite Rothschild, Chateau Latour and Chateau Margaux in quality and in 1855 it was awarded Second Growth status.

The 1844 vintage was the highest priced of any of the Second Growth wines of Margaux. Château Durfort-Vivens still retains strong ties with Chateau Margaux. For a period in the 20th century, its wines were made at Chateau Margaux and in an interesting development Château Durfort-Vivens now belongs to the Lurton family, who own Chateau Margaux.

The estate grows 65 percent Cabernet Sauvignon, 20 percent Merlot and 15 percent Cabernet Franc. However its grand vin, a classified Second Growth, is usually around 82 percent Cabernet Sauvignon and expresses prominent features of blackcurrant and cassis. It is drinkable from 5 years but best enjoyed after 10 years.

Château Lascombes (https://www.chateau-lascombes.com/) was originally the property of Durfort de Duras family who also owned Château Durfort-Vivens. In the 17th century it came to Antoine, chevalier de Lascombes through inheritance and his descendants owned the property until the French Revolution. In the early 20th century, it came to be owned by the Ginestet family holdings. During the latter part of World War Two, the estate served as Allied headquarters in the area. Although in total, Château Lascombes covers 84 hectares, this is fragmented in numerous parcels of vineyard throughout the appellation.

The estate grows 50 percent Merlot, 45 percent Cabernet Sauvignon and 5 percent Petit Verdot. From this is produced an elegant claret with a rich expression of blackcurrant. The wine, which was classified a Second Growth, develops an enhanced complexity as it ages. It is popular with wine collectors.

Pierre de Rauzan was a 17th century wine merchant who also served as estate manager at Château Latour in Pauillac. Using his expertise, he began to purchase land in the Medoc region. His huge estate in the Margaux appellation was subdivided after his death into four estates, Château Rauzan-Gassies, Château Rauzan-Ségla, Château Desmirail, and Château Marquis de Terme. Both Château Rauzan-Gassies and Château Rauzan-Ségla were awarded Second Growth status with the classification of 1855, while Château Desmirail achieved Third Growth status and Château Marquis de Terme achieved Fourth Growth status.

Château Rauzan-Ségla (http://www.chateaurauzansegla.com/) thrived under the able management of Marie-Anne de Rauzan, Eugene Durrand-Dassier and Frederic Cruse. After a period of decline, a new era began in the 1980s under guidance of leading wine researcher, Émile Peynaud.

The estate grows Cabernet Sauvignon and Merlot, with a small portion of Petit Verdot and Cabernet Franc. The grand vin ages well, expressing a spicy, floral aroma as it matures. Château Rauzan-Ségla produces a second wine, simply known as Ségla.

Château Rauzan-Gassies (http://www.domaines-quie.com/) also grows Cabernet Sauvignon, Merlot, Petit Verdot and Cabernet Franc. Unlike many Bordeaux wineries, the estate still uses machine harvesting.

Château Desmirail (http://www.desmirail.com/) came into the possession of Jean Desmirail as part of his wife's dowry and was acquired by Monsieur Sipière shortly before it was classified a Third Growth in 1855. Château Desmirail offers tours and tasting tours, but booking is advised.

Château Marquis de Terme, another of the Rauzan properties has been recently renovated and is in the process of conversion to organic farming practices.

Château Brane-Cantenac (http://www.brane-cantenac.com/en/) already had a reputation for producing wines of the Second Growth class prior to 1855. It is located to the west of the village Cantenac and from 1833 it belonged to Baron Hector de Branne who went by the moniker "Napoleon of Wines". After a period of decline, the winery was inherited by Lucien Lurton in 1956 and is currently owned and managed by Henri Lurton.

Château Brane-Cantenac grows 55 percent Cabernet Sauvignon, 40 percent Merlot, 4.5 percent Cabernet Franc and a small portion of Carmenère. The grand vin is characterized by the elegance of Margaux vintages. The estate produces a second wine, Baron de Brane, as well as a wine from its younger vines, Margaux de Brane.

Visitors can choose from a variety of experiences, ranging from a guided walk for €10 to gourmet tastings with cheese and wine.

Several notable Margaux estates are clustered around the village of Cantenac. **Château Kirwan** (http://www.chateau-kirwan.com/) was one of a handful of Bordeaux estates graced by a visit from wine lover Thomas Jefferson. It was acquired in 1710 by wine negociant, Sir John Collingwood, whose daughter married Irish merchant Mark Kirwan. The estate was later bequeathed to the City of Bordeaux. Its current owner is the negociant company, Schroder and Schyler.

Château Kirwan grows Cabernet Sauvignon, Merlot, Cabernet Franc and Petit Verdot. Besides the grand vin, a third growth, it produces a second wine, Les Charmes de Kirwan. The estate welcomes visitors and is particularly popular with Irish tourists.

According to historical record, wine from **Château d'Issan** (http://www.chateau-issan.com/en/) was served at the nuptials of Henry II and Eleanor of Aquitaine. This marked the beginning of England's love affair with wines from Bordeaux. Its moated chateau is one of the oldest in the Medoc. Notable owners in its long history include the Essenault family in the 16th century, the Foix de Candale family who owned it up to the French Revolution and the Cruse family who spearheaded its revival from the mid-20th century. Its wine was classified a Third Growth in 1855.

There are three more Third Growths in the vicinity of Cantenac. They are **Chateau Boyd-Cantenac** (http://www.boyd-cantenac.fr/english/), **Chateau Palmer** (http://www.chateau-palmer.com/) and **Chateau Cantenac-Brown** (http://www.cantenacbrown.com/), with its unique Tudor style chateau. Other nearby estates include **Chateau Pouget** (http://www.chateau-pouget.com/english/) and **Château Prieuré-Lichine** which are both Fourth Growths.

Château Ferrière (http://www.ferriere.com/) is barely 12 hectares but its terroir, which combines gravel and chalk marl, is ideal for growing Cabernet Sauvignon. The estate is named after the original owner, the Gabriel Ferrière family, who was the king's huntsman in the 18th century. His family owned the property until the early 20th century. It is currently run by Claire Villars-Lurton.

Château Giscours (http://www.chateau-giscours.fr/), which is located in the commune of Labarde, is one of the largest wineries in Margaux. According to historical record, it already existed as a fortified structure around 1330, but the first confirmed connection to wine making dates back to 1552.

The Third Growth estate passed through numerous owners and in the mid-1950s it was acquired by Nicholas Tari, an Algerian wine-maker who owned it until the 1990s. It is now owned by Alexander van Beek.

Château Giscours grows Cabernet Sauvignon, Merlot and Cabernet Franc, producing an aromatic, yet full-bodied grand vin. The 19th century chateau offers guest accommodation. Guided tours, wine tastings and wine workshops can be booked through the website.

Chateau Marquis d'Alesme

(https://www.marquisdalesme.wine/en/home) dates back to the 16th century and its first vines were planted early in the 17th century. In 1855 it was classified a Third Growth.

Recent investment in new wine-making equipment is beginning to pay off in the quality of its latest vintages. Guided tours and tastings can be arranged by appointment. Chateau Marquis d'Alesme is one of the few estates that also offer a child-friendly experience for young visitors.

Château Malescot-St.-Exupéry

(http://www.malescot.com/) dates back to the 18th century. In 1955 the Zuger family purchased the estate in a run-down condition. Through hard work, they managed to rebuild its reputation for quality. The smooth grand vin is at its best after 6 to 7 years of aging. There is a second wine, La Dame de Malescot.

Margaux has two classified Fifth Growths. **Chateau du Tertre** (http://chateaudutertre.fr/en/home/) dates back to the 12th century and during the 1700s it was owned by Pierre Mitchell, the well-known glass blower who also developed the jeroboam bottle. Today, the estate offers guided visits, tastings and holiday accommodation at its chateau.

Chateau Dauzac (http://www.chateaudauzac.com/) is located near the southern end of Margaux and dates back to the 17th century. After a period of decline it was purchased by Felix Chatellier in 1978 when a period of renovation began.

Visits, guided tours and tastings can be arranged and there is also a picnic area near one of its historical structures and an arboretum with several rare tree species. The estate makes honey on site. Its rooms can be rented for private functions, receptions and other events.

Saint Julien

St Julien is located on the Left Bank of the Gironde Estuary. Wedged between Pauillac and Margaux, it is only 920 acres. It is home to 11 Classified Growths and its wines are often regarded as similar to those of Pauillac. They have a deep, intense character and require a few years of aging before they can be approached.

Château Léoville Las Cases (http://www.domaines-delon.com/en/leoville-chateau_leoville_las_cases_vins.html) has a long history that goes back to the 17th century. Originally part of Domaine de Léoville which was owned by an influential noble family, it came into the ownership of the Las Cases family after the French Revolution. Currently it belongs to Jean Hubert Delon, who also owns Château Pontesac in Medoc and Château Nénin in Pomerol.

The vineyards comprise of 65 percent Cabernet Sauvignon, 19 percent Merlot, 13 percent Cabernet Franc and 3 percent Petit Verdot. Château Léoville Las Cases uses a process of reverse osmosis to remove excess water from the grapes during rainy seasons.

Its primary wine, Grand Vin de Léoville du Marquis de Las Cases was classified one of the original fifteen Deuxièmes Crus or Second Growths. It is the most expensive wine from the Saint Julien appellation, but is also widely regarded by experts as one of its finest. The chateau produces two other wines, Clos du Marquis under a separate label since 1902 and Le Petit Lion de Marquis de Las Cases. Château Léoville Las Cases lies at the northern border of Saint Julien and borders Château Latour in Pauillac.

Château Léoville-Poyferré (http://www.leoville-poyferre.fr/en/) resulted from the division of Domaine de Léoville after the French Revolution and the subsequent subdivision of one of those portions, Château Léoville Las Cases in 1840. It is currently run by Didier Cuvelier.

Château Léoville-Poyferré is blessed with well-drained gravel soil and its grapes consist of 65 percent Cabernet Sauvignon, 23 percent Merlot, 8 percent Petit Verdot and 4 percent Cabernet Franc.

The signature wine is Château Léoville-Poyferré, one of the original Deuxiemes Crus or Second Growths of 1855. Elegant and well-balanced, it is characterized by its intense color and excellent aging potential. Two additional wines are produced on Château Léoville-Poyferré. Pavillon de Léoville-Poyferré is a fruity wine that is easy on the palate. The subtle tannins of Château Moulin Riche blend Cabernet Sauvignon with Merlot which produces a wine that can be enjoyed at a younger age.

Tours and tastings at Château Léoville-Poyferré can be booked by phone or email. The facility is also available to be booked for seminars and other events. Personalized souvenirs can be purchased when visiting.

Château Léoville Barton (http://www.leoville-barton.com/en/) was once part of the huge Léoville estate. In 1826 it was purchased by the Irish-born Barton family who own it to this day. In 1855, it became a classified Second Growth.

Throughout six generations of Bartons, dedication to quality has remained consistent. Château Léoville Barton grows 72 percent Cabernet Sauvignon, 20 percent Merlot and 8 percent Cabernet Franc. Its wine is tannic when young, but matures to express elements of blackcurrant, cassis and cedar. The wines are produced at its sister property, **Chateau Langoa Barton**, a Third Growth which is also owned by the Barton family. Chateau Langoa Barton produces a second wine, Lady Langoa.

Château Ducru-Beaucaillou (http://www.chateau-ducru-beaucaillou.com/) is one of the oldest wineries in the Medoc, its history dating back to the 13th century. From 1720 the château was owned by the Bergeron family who sold the estate to Bertrand Ducru in 1795. In 1866, ownership passed to the Johnstons, and in the early 20th century to the Desbarats family. In 1941 it was acquired by the Borie family, who are associated with several other estates in Bordeaux.

Château Ducru-Beaucaillou presents visitors with unique views of the Gironde Estuary, its Victorian style chateau and the surrounding backdrop of a lovely park.

The estate grows 70 Cabernet Sauvignon and 30 percent Merlot. Grapes are harvested by hand and fermented in vats dedicated to specific plots of its terroir. The wine, which achieved Second Growth status in 1855, is powerful, rich in color, yet masterfully balanced. It is best drunk after 10 years of aging.

Château Gruaud-Larose (http://www.gruaud-larose.com/) dates from 1725 when it was founded by a knight called Joseph Stanislas Gruaud. He erected the tower, from which harvesting workers could be watched and where a flag was raised after the harvest to attract interested buyers.

In subsequent generations the property was subdivided but in the early 20th century the two fragmented estates were purchased by the Cordier family and reunited.

Château Gruaud-Larose grows 65 percent Cabernet Sauvignon, 25 percent Merlot, 8 percent Cabernet Franc and 2 percent Petit Verdot. When properly aged, its grand vin (a second growth) is characterized by a combination of black fruits, liquorice, spice and cedar.

A group tour of the estate can be booked for €10 per person and the Chateau offers several other immersive experiences including a tasting class, a harvest workshop and a cooking class.

Château Lagrange (http://chateau-lagrange.com/en/) is one of the largest vineyards in St Julien. In 1983, it was acquired by the Japanese liquor brand Suntory, who invested heavily in its makeover. The grand vin is a Third Growth and the estate also produces a second wine as well as a limited quantity of dry white wine.

Château Lagrange grows Cabernet Sauvignon, Merlot and Petit Verdot for its reds and Sauvignon Blanc, Semillon and Sauvignon Gris for its white wine.

The galley on the labels of **Château Beychevelle** (http://beychevelle.com/) wine is deeply symbolic, as one of the estate's former owners was Jean-Louis Nogaret de la Valette, Duke of Eperon and Admiral of France. Its name is derived from the phrase "Baisse Voile", which means 'lower the sails' and remembers the tradition for ships passing the estate who lowered their sails as a sign of respect.

The estate is known for its beautiful chateau and decorative gardens offering visitors stunning views of the Gironde. It was originally constructed in 1565 by Bishop François of Foix-Candale.

As dedicated patrons of the arts, the estate's owners host an annual art exhibition in partnership with Mécénart and regularly serves as venue for classical and jazz music concerts.

The facilities at La Table de Beychevelle are available for receptions, functions and conferences. Château Beychevelle grows Cabernet Sauvignon, Merlot, Cabernet Franc and Petit Verdot to produce its grand vin, a Fourth Growth, as well as a second wine, Admiral de Beychevelle. It applies organic and sustainable farming practices that promote biodiversity in the area.

Chateau Talbot (http://chateau-talbot.com/) was named after a 15th century British hero who served as the governor of the locality then known as Guyenne. Under the ownership of the Marquis of Aux, it was classified a Fourth Growth and from the early 20th century, it belonged to the Cordier family.

The estate grows 66 percent Cabernet Sauvignon, 26 percent Merlot, 5 percent Petit Verdot and 3 percent Cabernet Franc. Grapes are harvested by hand and the Genodics system is used to stimulate growth by emitting beneficial sounds and frequencies. At its best, the grand vin develops into an aromatic wine with characteristics of cedar wood, vanilla and cassis.

A portion of the vineyard is dedicated to growing Sauvignon Blanc and Semillon grapes to produce a white wine named Le Caillou Blanc. It is one of the few white wines cultivated in St Julien.

The origins of **Chateau Saint Pierre** (http://www.domaines-henri-martin.com/en/chateau-saint-pierre) go back to the latter part of the 17th century when the first vines were planted. In 1767, it was acquired by Baron de Saint Pierre and after his death, the property was subdivided and fell into decline. During the early part of the 20th century, the property was reunited and in 1982 it was sold to Henri Martin, a former mayor of St Julien.

Chateau Saint-Pierre, a Fourth Growth, grows 70 percent Cabernet Sauvignon, 20 percent Merlot and 10 percent Cabernet Franc. Its Grand vin is fragrant with a taste of cassis.

Henri Martin also created his own winery, **Château Gloria** (http://www.domaines-henri-martin.com/en/chateau-gloria) from the initial purchase of 6 hectares of land that had belonged to Chateau Saint Pierre. He slowly added land from other surrounding classed estates. Château Gloria was included in a proposed reclassification by renowned Russian-born wine writer, Alexis Lichine. It now comprises 50 hectares at the northern end of St Julien, bordering Pauillac.

Château Gloria grows 65 percent Cabernet Sauvignon, 25 percent Merlot, 5 percent Cabernet Franc and 5 percent Petit Verdot. Besides the Grand Vin, Château Gloria produces a secondary wine, Chateau Peymartin. Chateau Saint Pierre and Château Gloria are now administrated by Jean-Louis Triaud.

The Bourgeois Cru wines grown in St Julien include Château du Glana, Château Moulin de la Rose, Château Lalande Borie, Château Teynac and Château Bridane.

Saint Estephe

Saint-Estèphe is the northern-most appellation in the Medoc and is one of its largest at 1,377 hectares. While it is home to only five classified growths it has a large concentration of Cru Bourgeois wineries. Currently there are 35 chateaux in St Estephe that belong to this class.

The cooler climate results in a late harvest for this area. There is a significant clay component to its soil and in recent years, the appellation has increased its cultivation of Merlot grapes.

Château Montrose (http://www.chateau-montrose.com/en/) is located on a gravel knoll to the north of the tiny village of Marbuzet. Its fame was determined by three families. Etienne Théodore Dumoulin planted the first vineyards in a tract of land his family had acquired from Nicolas Alexandre de Ségur. Forty years later his wines were awarded Second Growth status in the 1855 classification.

In 1866 the estate came into the possession of Mathieu Dollfus. He modernized the winery, but also pioneered good social living standards and free healthcare for his workers. One of his innovations was the installation of a windmill to combat phylloxera. He also invested in the nearby village of Montrose.

From the late 1800s to 2006, the Charmolüe family continued in this proud tradition. The estate is currently managed by Hervé Berland. Recent renovations have solidified the estate's commitment to energy efficient operations.

Château Montrose grows 65 percent Cabernet Sauvignon, 25 percent Merlot and 10 percent Cabernet Franc and produces a powerful, full-bodied wine with great aging potential. Besides the grand vin, Château Montrose produces a second wine called La Dame de Montrose. A third wine, Saint-Estèphe de Montrose, is made from younger vines and can be enjoyed at an earlier stage.

Château Cos d'Estournel (http://estournel.com/) is located at the southern end of St Estephe near the prestigious Château Lafite Rothschild in neighbouring Pauillac. It was named in 1810 by Louis-Gaspard d'Estournel who also built the oriental style chateau on the property.

The estate changed ownership numerous times and for much of the 20th century, it belonged to the Ginestet family. The current owner is Michel Reybier.

Château Cos d'Estournel grows 60 percent Cabernet Sauvignon, 38 percent Merlot and 2 percent Cabernet Franc. The grapes are hand-picked after which they pass through a cooling tunnel into gravity cellars. The grand vin (a Second Growth) is full-bodied and tannic, increasing in intensity and complexity as it ages. The estate also produces an excellent second wine, Les Pagodes de Cos. Wines from Château Marbuzet, Goulée and Goulée Blanc are also produced by the same team of wine makers. To arrange a visit, use the contact form on the website.

Château Calon-Ségur (http://www.calon-segur.fr/en/) is the northernmost of the classified growths and is one of the oldest wineries in the Medoc. It is first mentioned in historical record around 1147 when it was owned by a local bishop. In the 18th century, it became the property of the Marquis de Ségur, Bordeaux's Prince of Wines who also left his mark on Chateau Latour, Chateau Lafite and Chateau Mouton. Château Calon-Ségur was awarded Third Growth status. It was owned by the Gasqueton family until 2012 and a charming feature is the stone wall that surrounds the vineyard. Château Calon-Ségur is currently managed by Laurent Dufau.

The estate grows 53 percent Cabernet Sauvignon, 38 percent Merlot 7 percent Cabernet Franc and 2 percent Petit Verdot. In recent years the grand vin has developed a soft and fruity character. There is a second wine, Marquis de Calon which has a higher percentage of Merlot.

Château Lafon-Rochet (http://www.lafon-rochet.com/) was founded in 1650 after the marriage of Pierre de Lafon and Antoinette de Guillemotte and remained in the family for more than 200 years. After a period of decline the château was acquired by the Tesseron family in 1960. Château Lafon-Rochet is a classified Fourth Growth. As with many wines in St Estephe, its character has been overly tannic in the past, but a shift towards a greater Merlot content has resulted in a more elegant wine.

The estate grows 56 percent Cabernet Sauvignon, 40 percent Merlot and 4 percent Cabernet Franc.

Château Cos-Labory (http://www.cos-labory.com/) has produced wine since the late 1700s and was classified a Fifth Growth in 1855. Its wines have a relatively high percentage of Cabernet Franc (roughly a third), which is blended with equal portions of Merlot and Cabernet Sauvignon.

Several wineries from St Estephe were awarded Cru Bourgeois Exceptionnels status in the controversial rating of 2003. These were **Château Ormes de Pez**, **Chateau de Pez**, **Chateau Haut Marbuzet** and Château Phélan Ségur.

Château Phélan Ségur (http://www.phelansegur.com/) resulted from the 19th century merging of two estates, Clos de Garramey and Segur and is managed by Thierry Gardiner. The estate employs environmentally-sensitive operational approaches and alongside the grand vin produces two more wines, the Frank Phelan and La Croix Bonis. Visits and tastings can be booked on weekdays, all year round.

Of historical interest is **Chateau de Pez** (http://www.chateaudepez.com/en/), which dates back to the 15th century.

Chateau Meyney (http://www.meyney.fr/en/) dates back to the 17th century, when it was a convent and monks planted the first vines. Its wine enjoys the Cru Bourgeois classification.

Other Cru Bourgeois estates in St Estephe include **Chateau Le Crock** (http://chateaulecrock.fr/fr/), **Chateau La Boscq** (http://www.dourthe.com/en/vineyard/2-chateau-le-boscq), **Chateau Petit Bocq** (https://www.chateau-petit-bocq.com/), the recently renovated **Chateau Tronquoy Lalande** (http://www.tronquoy-lalande.com/), **Chateau Capbern Gasqueton**, **Chateau Lilian Ladouys** (http://www.chateau-lilian-ladouys.com/), **Chateau Haut Beausejour** and **Chateau La Commanderie** (http://catharchateau.com/en/), which can be booked for special events such as weddings.

Haut-Médoc

Haut-Médoc resulted from a bold initiative by Dutch merchants in the 17th century to drain the salt marshes along the Gironde River and convert them to vineyards. The investment paid off well. Within the area are four of Bordeaux's most prestigious appellations, namely Pauillac, Margaux, Saint Julien and Saint Estephe, as well as two smaller appellations, Listrac-Médoc and Moulis-en-Médoc. The Haut-Médoc, which covers everything not included in the other six, comprises nearly 400 wineries and produces over two million cases of wine.

The appellation was officially defined in 1936. Although it is the largest Left Bank Appellation, Haut-Médoc is home to only five classified growths. It also has a considerable number of Cru Bourgeois classified wineries.

Cru Bourgeois wineries worth exploring include Chateau Lanessan, Chateau Peyrabon, Chateau Saint Paul, Chateau de Gironville, Chateau Bernadotte and Chateau Charmail.

Château La Tour Carnet (http://www.bernard-magrez.com/en/wines/chateau-la-tour-carnet-0) is one of the oldest estates in the Medoc. At least one of its structures - a distinctive round tower - dates back to the 11th century and it served as a fortress for the English in the 12th century.

Towards the end of the 20th century the property was acquired by Bernard Magrez who was the founder of the William Pitters spirits company. He owns various other chateaux in Bordeaux. After taking over Château La Tour Carnet, Magrez increased the size of the vineyard and added a larger portion of Merlot grapes.

Besides the grand vin, a Fourth Growth, the estate produces Servitude Volontaire, which is made from 100 percent Merlot grapes. Recently, a dry white wine blended from Sauvignon Blanc, Semillon and Sauvignon Gris was introduced. Customized tasting tours can be booked. Château La Tour Carnet also offers luxury accommodation.

Château La Lagune (http://www.chateau-lalagune.com) dates from the 16th century and its lovely 18th century chateau was designed by the architect Baron Victor Louis. The estate experienced a period of decline after World War Two, but revived under the ownership of George Burnette. It is currently managed by Caroline Frey, whose family has owned it since 2000.

Château La Lagune grows Cabernet Sauvignon, Merlot and Petit Verdot. The grand vin, a Third Growth, is elegant, with a complex aroma. The estate produces a second wine, Moulin de la Lagune.

Château Cantemerle (http://www.cantemerle.com) dates from the 12th century. One of its previous owners fought at the Battle of Taillebourge as an ally of Henry III, while another served as the president of Bordeaux. The estate's vineyards date back to the 14th century. Château Cantemerle, a Fifth Growth, was the last classified in 1855 but accidentally excluded from the regional map at the 1855 exposition. The matter was rectified the next year. As one of the southernmost properties, it is one of the first that visitors encounter when touring the Medoc wine route.

Château de Camensac (www.chateaucamensac.com) and **Château Belgrave St.-Laurent**, the other two Fifth Growths are located near the commune of St Laurent.

Moulis AOC

Moulis is an appellation of 630 hectares located about halfway between Margaux and Saint Julien. It is located around the village Moulis-en-Médoc. This area grows primarily Cabenet Sauvignon, Merlot, Cabernet Franc, Carmenere and Petit Verdot. It produces red wine with a rich bouquet and has good aging potential. There are 31 wines produced in Moulis that bear Cru Bourgeois ranking and 13 wines with Cru Artisan rating.

Highly rated chateaux include Chateau Chasse Spleen (http://www.chasse-spleen.com/), Chateau Poujeaux (http://www.chateaupoujeaux.com/), Chateau Anthonic (http://www.chateauanthonic.com/index-en.html?lg=cn), Chateau Biston-Brillette (http://chateaubistonbrillette.fr/en/), Chateau Maucaillou (http://www.chateau-maucaillou.com/), Chateau Duplessis and Chateau Bel-Air Lagrave.

Listrac-Médoc AOC

The first vineyards of Listrac were planted in the 12th century and it became an appellation in the Medoc in 1957. Listrac-Médoc is home to 61 wineries of which 29 are rated Cru Bourgeois and 12 Cru Artisan. The area produces a robust red wine with a deep color and fruity aromas of blackcurrant, blackberry and plum.

Recommended chateaux include Château Clarke, Château Fonréaud (http://www.chateau-fonreaud.com/version-anglaise-fonreaud/index.html), Chateau Fourcas-Dupre (http://www.fourcasdupre.com/), Chateau Fourcas-Hosten (http://www.fourcas-hosten.fr/en/fourcas-hosten/10/history.html), Château Peyre-Lebade and Château Saransot-Dupre Listrac (http://www.saransot-dupre.com/?lang=en).

Graves

Graves was the region that first put Bordeaux wines on the map. As far back as the 12th century, the wine from Graves found a market in England. Queen Eleanor of Aquitaine was a fan.

Graves is the birthplace of claret and its output is the most varied of the Bordeaux regions with its reds, dry whites and sweet whites. Located to the southeast of the city of Bordeaux, Graves is subdivided into five appellations, namely Graves AOC, Graves Supérieures AOC, Pessac-Léognan AOC, Sauternes AOC & Barsac AOC and Cérons AOC.

Pessac-Leognan

Château Haut-Brion (https://www.haut-brion.com/) has a very long tradition of wine making. The land may have been used for vineyards as far back as the Roman era, but the first written record of its wines is in 1426.

The origins of the Haut-Brion of today can be found in the 1525 union of Jeanne de Bellon and Jean de Pontac, which included a tract of land in the dowry. Jean de Pontac commenced with the construction of a mansion and the planting of vines on the property's gravelly hillock.

This was to be the foundation of the oldest of the 1855 First Growths. Haut-Brion wines rose to prominence at a relatively early stage. Diarist Samuel Pepys mentions first tasting it in April 1663 at the Royal Oak Tavern in London. Other early fans were philosopher John Locke and Thomas Jefferson.

One of the estate's more celebrated past owners was the politician Charles Maurice de Talleyrand-Périgord, whose chef employed the wines in high-profile culinary duels with the rival chef of Austrian politician Metternich.

Early in the 20th century, Château Haut-Brion was purchased by American banker Clarence Dillon. It is currently run by one of his descendants, Prince Robert of Luxembourg.

Haut-Brion cultivates both red and white grapes. For its red wines, Haut-Brion grows 49 percent Merlot, 40 percent Cabernet Sauvignon, 10 percent Cabernet Franc and 1 percent Petit Verdot. The white grapes comprise 51.5 percent Sémillon and 48.5 percent Sauvignon Blanc, as well as a small portion of Sauvignon Gris.

The terroir consists of Gunzian gravel, which provides excellent drainage, with significant parcels of clay and vineyards can be found at an elevation of 27m. The nearness of the city Bordeaux promotes a slightly warmer microclimate and an early ripening of its grapes.

The wines are aged for 24 months in barrels of French oak and most of these are produced on site. The signature wine is Château Haut-Brion, one of the original five Premier Grand Cru or First Growths. There is a second red wine, Le Clarence de Haut-Brion, as well as two whites, Château Haut-Brion Blanc, a rare wine blended from Sémillon, Sauvignon Blanc and Sauvignon Gris and La Clarte de Haut-Brion. Château Haut-Brion can be visited by appointment only. See the website for details.

Château Pape Clément (http://www.bernard-magrez.com/en/wines/chateau-pape-clement) is one of the oldest vineyards in Bordeaux. It was gifted to Bernard de Goth around 1300, upon his appointment as Archbishop of Bordeaux. When Bernard later became Pope Clement V, he in turn gave the estate to his successor, a practice that continued until the French Revolution.

In 1939 the property was bought by Paul Montagne and today, his descendants are still involved in its operation.

Château Pape Clément produces both red and white wine. It grows 60 percent Cabernet Sauvignon and 40 percent Merlot for its red vintage. The white wines comprise a smaller portion of the property and include Semillon, Sauvignon Blanc, Sauvignon Gris and Muscadelle.

The estate uses solar powered drones to help monitor developments in the vineyards. Visits and wine tastings can be booked on the website. The 16th century castle on the estate is available for holiday accommodation. It offers free Wi-Fi, TV and private bathroom facilities. There is also a chapel and a gift shop.

Domaine de Chevalier (http://www.domainedechevalier.com/) belonged to the Ricard family from 1865 to 1983 when it was purchased by Oliver Bernard. The estate produces both red and white wine. For its grand vin, it grows 64 percent Cabernet Sauvignon, 30 percent Merlot, 3 percent Cabernet Franc and 3 percent Petit Verdot.

Five hectares are dedicated to the white, with 70 percent Sauvignon Blanc and 30 percent Semillon. Grapes are picked by hand and sorted in the vineyard. Visits can be arranged by appointment.

Chateau La Mission-Haut-Brion (http://www.mission-haut-brion.com/en/#/intro) dates back to the early 16th century. It was purchased by Jean de Pontac in 1533 and inherited by his niece Olive de Lestonnac in 1607. She in turn bequeathed it to Congregation of the Mission, making it the property of the Catholic Church. It remained until the French Revolution when it was confiscated by the state.

It belonged to the Woltner family for much of the 20th century. The estate was purchased by the owners of Domaine Clarence Dillon in 1983 when the facilities were modernized.

Its rich, powerful red wines are produced from Cabernet Sauvignon, Merlot and Cabernet Franc and best approached after at least ten years of aging. The estate also produces an excellent white wine from Semillon and Sauvignon Blanc.

To arrange a visit, fill in the request form on the website. From 2006, the harvest from **Chateau La Tour Haut-Brion** has been merged with the wines of Chateau La Mission Haut-Brion – its final vintage was 2005. **Chateau Laville Haut Brion**, which produces one of the finest dry whites in Bordeaux, also falls under the same ownership.

Chateau Smith Haut Lafitte (http://www.smith-haut-lafitte.com/en/smith-haut-lafitte-visite.html) is located on a gravel plateau. Its vineyards date from the 14th century when they were planted by the du Bosque family. The estate's manor house was constructed by its 17th century Scottish owner, Georges Smith.

In 1990 the estate was acquired by Olympic skier Daniel Cathiard, who modernized its facilities and designed an innovative transportation system for the grapes based on methods used by the Sherpas in Tibet.

The grand vin is a blend of Cabernet Sauvignon, Merlot and Cabernet Franc. Visitors can book various types of experiences. You can opt for basic tastings, a tasting initiation, where wines are paired with dried fruit or chocolate, a wine-making tour or an art and wine tour that showcases the chateau's art treasures.

Chateau Carbonnieux (http://carbonnieux.com/?lang=en) dates back to 1234 when it was founded by Ramon Carbonnieu. During its illustrious history, it entertained Thomas Jefferson. The estate grows Cabernet Sauvignon, Merlot, Sauvignon Blanc and Semillon. It is classified for both red and white wine. The estate is open to the public by appointment. A boutique shop sells wine, souvenirs, honey, grape jelly and books. There is also a permanent exhibition of antique cars, jugs and winemaking tools.

Château de Fieuzal (http://www.fieuzal.com/en/) produces a classified red, as well as an unclassified dry white and once supplied wine to the Vatican. **Chateau Couhins** (http://chateau-couhins.fr/en/) was acquired by Institut National de la Recherche Agronomique (INRA) in 1968 and forms an integral part of that organization's ongoing research in the development of sustainable wine growing practices. It uses green energy and utilizes GPS positioning in monitoring its vineyards. A portion of the estate was acquired by André Lurton, who created the separate entity of **Chateau Couhins Lurton** (http://eng.andrelurton.com/Our-Wines/Our-wines/Chateau-Couhins-Lurton-Blanc).

André Lurton has been involved in IMRA since the mid-1960s and played a leading role in various other regulatory bodies in the wine industry. One of his most significant achievements was the defining of Pessac-Léognan as a separate appellation within the greater region of Graves.

Chateau Olivier (http://www.chateau-olivier.com/) dates back to the 11th century although wine making only began centuries later. Both its red and white wines were classified in 1953.

Château Bouscaut (http://www.chateau-bouscaut.com/uk) dates back to the 18th century and both its red and white wines are classified growths. The estate was acquired by Lucien Lurton in 1979 and is currently managed by his daughter, Sophie. It grows Cabernet Sauvignon, Merlot, Malbec, Sémillon and Sauvignon blanc. The estate won a Wine Tourism award in 2013 for its workshops and a variety of other activities for tourists. These include cheese and wine tastings, food and wine pairings and even the opportunity to create your own wine blend, under the guidance of a professional oenologist.

Château Haut-Bailly (https://www.chateau-haut-bailly.com/en) produces a small quantity of rosé in addition to its classed red wine. **Château Latour-Martillac** is named for a 12th century tower, the only structure remaining of a castle that once stood on the property. It is classified for its red and white wines. Its Semillon vines are over a century old, making them the oldest of that grape type in Bordeaux. **Château Malartic-Lagravière** (http://www.malartic-lagraviere.com/en/) is likewise classified for its red and white wines. It also produces a rosé wine, Le Rosé de Malartic. The chateau is available for the hosting of events and functions.

Sauternes

Sauternes is located about 40km southeast of Bordeaux in the Graves region, in the proximity of the Garonne and Cirron Rivers. The presence of the cooler Cirron promotes the frequent occurrence of mist and this in turn makes its vineyards highly susceptible to noble rot, a beneficial fungus infection that sweetens grapes grown in this area. Sauternes includes the communes of Barsac, Bommes, Preignac and Forgues.

Château d'Yquem (http://yquem.fr/int-en/) can be found on the highest hill in the Sauternes appellation. A significant factor of the production is the careful cultivation and observation of Botrytis infection also known as noble rot.

The estate's history can be traced back to 1477 when it was acquired by Ramon Felipe Eyquem a merchant in wine and herring. In 1593, the estate came into the possession of the De Sauvage family and they married into the Lur Saluces around 1785. It was during this period that the sweet wines they produce, came to the notice of wine connoisseur and US diplomat Thomas Jefferson, who named it the finest white wine in all of France.

In 2006 a bottle from the collection sold for $100,000 at auction and in 2011 an 1811 vintage sold for $117,000. It is the only white wine from Bordeaux to be awarded *Premier Cru Superiur* or Superior First Growth status.

Château d'Yquem grows 80 percent Semillon and 20 percent Sauvignon Blanc and produces sweet, complex wines with good potential for aging. The wine is more expensive than most other whites in the region. The best Château d'Yquem vintages have an aging potential of up to 50 years.

Grapes are harvested by hand and at different stages of Botrytis infection, a strategy that affords the wine its uniquely layered taste, but comes at a heavy cost of labor and yield. The wine is golden-hued and darkens with age. When young, it expresses flavors of honey and tropical fruit. With aging, flavors of caramel and spice are more evident.

A 90 minute guided tour can be booked for €60. Tasting is included.

There are several classified white wines produced near the village of Bommes. The First Growth chateau include Château La Tour Blanche, Château Lafaurie-Peyraguey, Château Clos Haut-Peyraguey, Château de Rayne-Vigneau, Château Rabaud-Promis and Château Sigalas-Rabaud.

Château La Tour Blanche (http://www.tour-blanche.com/) dates back to the 18th century when it was the property of Jean Saint-Marc du Latourblanche, treasury general of Louis XIV. The estate flourished when German winemaker Frederic Focke applied traditions from the Rhone Valley to his wines. After his death, Daniel "Osiris" Iffla purchased the property and donated it to the French state. It houses the La Tour Blanche School of Viticulture and Oenology. The purpose of this institution is to educate the winemakers of the future. The estate grows 83 percent Semillon, 12 percent Sauvignon Blanc and 5 percent Muscadelle. The grand vin is powerful and exotic, with great aging potential. The estate produces a second wine, Les Charmilles de La Tour Blanche, as well as several dry whites and a red from Merlot and Malbec. Château La Tour Blanche is open to the public for guided tours and gourmet visits. You can also book for lunch and enjoy its selection of food/wine pairings.

Château Rabaud-Promis and Château Sigalas-Rabaud were once part of a larger estate, Château Rabaud, which dates back to the 1600s when it was owned by the de Cazeau family. The properties were divided in 1913, but reunited in the 1930s, under the tenancy of Fernand Ginestet. In the 1950s, the two properties were separated once more.

Château Sigalas-Rabaud (http://www.chateau-sigalas-rabaud.com/) is currently run by Laure de Lambert Compeyrot. **Château Rabaud-Promis** (http://rabaud-promis.com/z/site.php?act=4) was sold to the Dejean family, who still own it. Visits and tastings can be booked by appointment. **Chateau de Rayne Vigneau** (http://www.raynevigneau.fr/en/), a First Growth winery, overlooks the nearby Ciron river. Besides regular visits and tastings, the estate also offers visitors the opportunity to explore the vineyards on horseback.

Chateau Clos Haut Peyraguey (http://www.bernard-magrez.com/en/wines/chateau-clos-haut-peyraguey) and Chateau Lafaurie Peyraguey were once part of the same hillside estate, which was acquired by LaFaurie after the French Revolution. In 1879, when it was owned by the Duchatel family, the property was divided into two, with the highest vineyards becoming Chateau Clos Haut Peyraguey, while the lower vineyards being named Chateau Lafaurie Peyraguey. Chateau Clos Haut Peyraguey was run by the Garbay family for almost a century, before it was acquired in 2012 by Bernard Magrez, who owns numerous properties in Bordeaux as well as Languedoc-Rousillon, Spain, Portugal, South America, California, Morocco and Japan.

Chateau Clos Haut Peyraguey grows 95 percent Semillon and 5 percent Sauvignon Blanc. Besides the Grand Vin, the estate produces two more wines, Chateau Haut Bommes and Symphonie de Haut Peyraguey.

The chateau at **Chateau Lafaurie Peyraguey** (http://www.chateau-lafaurie-peyraguey.com/) dates back to the 13th century, when it served as fortification. At the time of the 1855 classification, its wines were ranked third after those of Château d'Yquem and Château La Tour Blanche. From 1917 to 1984, it belonged to the Cordier family. In 2014 the property was acquired by Silvio Denz.

The estate grows 93 percent Semillon, 6 percent Sauvignon Blanc and 1 percent Muscadelle. Besides the grand vin, there is a second wine, La Chapelle de Lafaurie Peyraguey as well as a dry white.

The vineyards of **Château Guiraud** (http://chateauguiraud.fr/en/) are located on a hill overlooking the village of Sauternes. The estate dates back to at least 1766 when it was purchased by a Protestant wine merchant, Pierre Guiraud.

Its wine was awarded Premier Cru status among white wines in 1855. In 2006, the estate was purchased by a partnership that includes Robert Peugeot, Oliver Bernhard, who owns Domaine de Chevalier, Stephan Von Neipperg, who is associated with several wineries around St Emilion and Xavier Planty, the estate's manager. They modernized the facility and switched to a regime of environmentally sustainable farming practices.

The estate grows 65 percent Semillon and 35 percent Sauvignon Blanc. The grand vin is refreshing, yet rich and complex. It is particularly suitable for pairing with shellfish or foie gras.

Visits can be arranged on most days except over Christmas or Easter. A guided tour plus tasting costs €12 per person and can be booked online.

Other classified wineries in Sauternes includes **Château Filhot** (http://www.filhot.com/chateau-filhot-sauternes-second-growth-classified-in-1855-4001.dhtml) - another favorite of Thomas Jefferson, **Château d'Arche** (http://chateau-arche.com/), **Château Romer du Hayot** (http://vignobles-du-hayot.com/en/) and **Château Lamothe-Guignard** (http://chateau-lamothe-guignard.fr/sautern.html).

There are two classified wineries around the commune of Preignac. **Chateau Suduiraut** (http://www.suduiraut.com/en/) is located right next to Château d'Yquem, the most prestigious property in Sauternes. The estate dates back to the wedding of Leonard de Suduiraut and Nicole d'Allard in 1580 and saw a renovation period under Count Blaise de Suduiraut in the 17th century. It was classified a First Growth in 1855. It is now managed by Pierre Christian Seely. Private tours can be arranged by appointment. The estate also arranges aroma workshops and tasting menus.

Chateau de Malle (http://www.chateaudemalle.fr/) has been owned by the Lur Saluces family, who were also associated with Château d'Yquem, for almost 250 years. It was classified as a Second Growth in 1855. It is now owned and managed by the Comtesse de Bournazel and her sons. The estate grows Semillon, Sauvignon Blanc and Muscadelle grapes.

Château Rieussec (http://www.lafite.com/en/the-chateaus/chateau-rieussec/) is located in the village of Fargues and was once run by a community of Carmelite monks. After the French Revolution the property had several owners before it was acquired by Domaines Barons de Rothschild in 1984. Its wine was classified as a First Growth in 1855. The estate produces a richly exotic sweet wine with the potential to match Château d'Yquem in quality. Its 2001 vintage won the Wine Spectator's Wine of the Year award in 2004. Tours and visits can be booked by appointment.

Barsac

Barsac lies between Sauternes and Ciron River. Its terroir of reddish soil produces wines that can be drier and more light-bodied than usual for the Sauternes appellation. For this reason, wineries in the region will also use the Barsac Appellation for labelling.

Barsac has two First Growth wineries. **Chateau Climens** (http://www.chateau-climens.fr/en/) is located near the village, La Pinesse. The estate was first mentioned in historical record in 1547 and was classified a First Growth in 1855. It is currently owned by the Lurton family.

Chateau Climens grows 100 percent Semillon grapes and produces a wine that can be described as graceful and complex.

Château Coutet (http://www.chateaucoutet.com/) produces wines that are rich and concentrated. The estate has several historical structures, such as a 13th century tower and a 14th century chapel. Besides the grand vin, a First Growth, the estate produces a second wine, Chartreuse de Coutet and a dry white, Vin Sec de Château Coutet. There is also an extremely rare fourth wine, Cuvée Madame de Château Coutet, produced from the oldest parcels of land and named after Madame Rolland-Guy, who ran the estate for over 50 years. Cuvée Madame de Château Coutet is only produced in select years and seldom in quantities larger than 1,000 bottles.

As the names suggest, Château Doisy Daëne, Château Doisy-Védrines and Château Doisy-Dubroca were once part of the same estate. They were divided in 1851. All three wineries are classified Second Growths. **Château Doisy Daëne** is named for its owner in the late-1800s, Jacques Emmanuel Daëne. In 1924 it was acquired by the Dubourdieu family. Denis Dubourdieu was a professor of oenology at the University of Bordeaux. The estate is currently managed by his sons.

Château Doisy-Védrines, the largest of the three, is the only one that uses the Sauternes, rather than Barsac appellation for labelling. Its grand vin is a rich, full-bodied sweet white made from Semillon, Sauvignon Blanc and Muscadelle. The estate also produces a dry white.
Château Doisy-Dubroca was previously owned by the Lurton family, but was purchased in 2014 by Denis Dubourdieu. Some of its vineyards have been incorporated with Château Doisy Daëne. The estate will produce no further vintages under its own label.

Chateau de Myrat (http://chateaudemyrat.fr/index.php/en/) was founded in the 1700s and rose to prominence under the Demerit family. In 1937, it was acquired by the de Pontac family, who are associated with Chateau Haut Brion and various other prestigious wineries. The estate grows Semillon, Sauvignon Blanc and Muscadelle and produces sweet wine with characteristics of honey, vanilla and citrus. Chateau de Myrat is a classified Second Growth.

Chateau Nairac (http://www.chateaunairac.com/) was founded in the 1700s by Elysee Nairac and currently owned and managed by Nicholas Heeter. The estate is a classified Second Growth but compares favorably with First Growths in the region. The produce of **Chateau Broustet** was once labelled Chateau Broustet-Nairac, as it was previously owned by the same family as Chateau Nairac. **Chateau Caillou** (http://www.chateaucaillou.com/) has belonged to the Ballan family from 1909 and produces a Second Growth with characteristics of honey, cinnamon and citrus.

Cerrons AOC

Cerrons is a small appellation to the north of Barsac which produces sweet, botrytized white wines. It consists mainly of three communes, Cerrons, Illsats and Podensac. The best known estates are Chateau de Cerons (http://www.chateaudecerons.com/the-wines/), Chateau Laroche Jaubert and Chateau de Chantegrive, which at 97 hectares is one of the largest estates in Graves. Podensac is also known for producing Lillet, an aromatized wine aperitif.

Right Bank Appellations

St Emilion

St Emilion has been growing vines since the 2nd century AD. This picturesque village with its charming medieval character, narrow, cobbled streets and underground catacombs is home to over 800 wineries. Besides ancient wine estates there are Romanesque churches dating back to the 12th century and access is via the seven gates that formed part of the original fortification. Saint Emilion's richly layered history has earned it a declaration as UNESCO world heritage site. Today it produces a large diversity of wines. There are four satellite appellations, namely Lussac Saint Emilion (which includes the former satellite Parsec Saint Emilion), Montagne Saint Emilion, Puisseguin Saint Emilion and Saint Georges St. Emilion.

Only four estates in St Emilion carry the Premiers Grands Crus Classés (A) classification. They are Château Angelus, Château Ausone, Château Pavie and Château Cheval Blanc. Two of these, Château Ausone and Château Pavie date from Roman times.

Château Angélus (http://www.angelus.com/en/) is one of the largest estates in St Emilion and its wine was awarded Premier grand cru classé (A) in the St Emilion Classification of 2012. It was founded in 1782 by Georges de Bouard, whose family had been active in the Bordeaux region since at least the 14th century. Today, the estate is owned by the same family and currently managed by Hubert de Bouard. Château Angélus grows 50 percent Merlot, 47 percent Cabernet Franc and 3 percent Cabernet Sauvignon. Grapes are destemmed by hand. The wine is approachable after 5 years of aging.

Château Cheval Blanc (http://www.chateau-cheval-blanc.com/en/) was founded when 15 hectares belonging to Chateau Figeac was sold to M. Loussac-Fourcaud in 1832. The estate rose to prominence when it won medals at the International Exhibitions of London (1862) and Paris (1867). The wine also featured in various popular culture references - James Bond drinks it in the movie 'Never Say Never Again'. It leaves a velvet feel in the mouth and a symphony of delicate flavors.

Unlike the majority of Right Bank wineries, the estate grows 57 percent Cabernet Franc, 40 percent Merlot and 3 percent Malbec. Besides the grand vin, a Premier grand cru classé (A), there is a second wine Petit Cheval Blanc. Château Cheval Blanc remained in the same family until 1998, when it was sold to Bernard Arnault and Albert Frere. It is currently managed by Pierre Lurton.

The name, **Château Pavie** (http://www.vignoblesperse.com/en/) recalls a peach orchard that once grew in this area. The winery was acquired in 1998 by Gérard Perse who was a former professional cyclist. Château Pavie grows Merlot, Cabernet Franc and Cabernet Sauvignon and produces a rich and concentrated blend with a fruity bouquet. The estate can be visited by appointment. An hour-long private tour culminates in a tasting session and costs €35.

Château Ausone (http://www.chateau-ausone.fr/) is located on a steep hillside just south of St Emilion. The estate is named after the Roman statesman and poet Decimius Magnus Ausonius, who lived in the 4th century AD and who owned a vineyard in Bordeaux. While it is uncertain whether the property can be positively identified as his, there are the remains of a Roman villa at the lower end. Château Ausone belonged to the Lescours family from the 13th to the 16th century. Currently it is managed by Alain Vauthier, whose family has long been associated with the property (since the late 17th century). The estate grows Merlot and Cabernet Franc.

Château Beauséjour and Chateau Beausejour Becot were once part of the same estate. In medieval times, the vineyard was worked by the monks of the Church of St-Martin. In 1869, Pierre-Paulin Ducarpe divided the property between his two children. **Château Beauséjour** (https://chateau-beausejour.com/), also known as Château Beauséjour-Duffau-Lagarrosse went to his daughter, who married Doctor Duffau-Lagarrosse. The Duffau-Lagarrosse family still own and operate the estate. The château grows Merlot, Cabernet Franc and Cabernet Sauvignon. The wine is powerful and full-bodied with characteristics of black fruit and spice. It is best approached after 6 to 7 years of aging.

The son inherited **Chateau Beau-Sejour Becot** (http://www.beausejour-becot.com/) and sold it to Dr Fagouet in 1924. In 1969, it was acquired by Michel Bécot, whose family continues to run the château. The estate grows 70 percent Merlot, 24 percent Cabernet Franc and 6 percent Cabernet Sauvignon. In 1985 the wine was demoted from Premier Grand Cru Classé to Grand Cru Classé as it operated two non-classed vineyards. Since 1996 the wine has been reinstated to its previous status however.

At 40 hectares, **Château Figeac** (http://www.chateau-figeac.com/) is the largest estate in St Emilion. The property is connected to a Gallo-Roman winery that dates back to the 2nd century AD and was named after a certain Figeacus. In the 18th century, the estate was huge - almost 200 hectares - but after several subdivisions, it was reduced to the current size. For a large part of the 20th century, the estate was run by Thierry Manoncourt, who was active in several Bordeaux wine associations including the Bordeaux Grand Crus Union and the Jurade of St. Emilion.

With a significant amount of gravel in the terroir, Château Figeac grows equal portions of Merlot, Cabernet Sauvignon and Cabernet Franc and produces a vintage that is reminiscent of the style of Medoc.

Chateau Canon (http://www.chateaucanon.com/en/) was originally part of a small vineyard planted by the religious community of Clos St-Martin and was acquired by the privateer, Jacques Kanon in 1760. Its terroir is particularly interesting. Beneath the topsoil of clay and limestone lie a network of limestone caves that were quarried for building material in the area. The estate grows Merlot and Cabernet Franc and produces wines with a silky style and good aging potential.

Château La Gaffelière (http://www.chateau-la-gaffeliere.com/) was once part of the same estate as Château Cannon-La Gaffelière. It includes the ruins of a Gallo-Roman villa and the name comes from the 17th century when it was a leper colony. It has been the property of the Malet-Roquefort family - who built its Gothic style chateau - for 300 years. The estate grows 65 percent Merlot, 30 percent Cabernet Franc and 5 percent Cabernet Sauvignon.

Clos Fourtet (http://www.closfourtet.com/) is located opposite St Emilion's main gate and once served as a fortification for the village. Its winemaking dates from the 18th century. Clos Fourtet was previously owned by the Ginestet family and the Lurton family. It currently is owned by Philippe Cuvelier.

Chateau Pavie Marquin (http://www.pavie-macquin.com/en/saint-emilion/actualites/) lies east of St Emilion on the Côte Pavie. It was named after Albert Marquin who was a pioneer in the struggle against phylloxera. Since the early 1990s it has been operated by Nicholas Thienpoint and consultant Stephane Derenoncourt who employ biodynamic winemaking practices.

Thienpoint and Derenoncourt are also responsible for **Chateau Larcis Ducasse** (http://www.larcis-ducasse.com/saint-emilion/actualites/). The estate was highly rated in centuries past. Lecoutre de Beauvais spoke highly of the château and in 1867 it was awarded a gold medal at the International Exposition in Paris. The terroir benefits from its consistency of clay, chalk, limestone and alluvial sand deposits.

Chateau Trotte Vielle is one of the older wineries in the area and currently belongs to Borie Manoux, the same negociant firm who run Chateau Lynch-Moussas and Chateau Batailley. The name means "trotting old lady" and recalls a gossiper from centuries past.

Chateau La Dominique (http://en.chateau-ladominique.com/) dates from the 17th century and was owned by the Chaperon family from 1788 to 1850. In the mid-20th century it was acquired by Clement Fayat. He added a modern winery designed by French architect Jean Nouvel with a rooftop restaurant famed in the area for its excellent cheese and wine platters. You can enjoy panoramic views of the vineyards. A tour of the winery includes a guided tasting, but tasting workshops or a food and wine experience can also be booked. Chateau La Dominique grows predominantly Merlot, with a small portion of Cabernet Franc and Cabernet Sauvignon. Its wine has a fruity aroma with an undertone of spice.

Château Troplong Mondot (http://www.chateau-troplong-mondot.com/) goes back to the 17th century when it became the property of Abbe Raymond de Seze. The de Seze family built its charming chateau in 1745 and in 1850 was acquired by Raymond Troplong. It is currently owned by the Valette family. With its attractive hilltop location overlooking the village of St Emilion, it is one of the larger estates in the area. Under the management of Xavier Pariente, Château Troplong Mondot has adopted organic farming practices.

It grows 90 percent Merlot, 5 percent Cabernet Franc and 5 percent Cabernet Sauvignon. The grand vin was awarded Premier Grand Cru Classé B in the 2012 St Emilion classification. The estate produces a second wine, simply called Mondot. The restaurant at Château Troplong Mondot offers optimized food and wine combinations, as tailored by chef David Charrier.

In recent years, Saint Emilion has become a hotbed for a controversial new trend in winemaking. The Garagistes are a group of up-and-coming winemakers who challenge some of the traditional methods and ideas of Bordeaux wine. The movement began in the 1990s when Jean-Luc Thunevin and Murielle Andraud purchased a hectare of land in St Emilion and converted it into the micro-winery of **Chateau Valandraud** (http://www.thunevin.com/chateau-valandraud). Its first vintage was limited to 100 cases but when their 1995 vintage received a stellar rating from wine expert Robert Parker, the price and demand for Chateau Valandraud rose rapidly. Out of this rags-to-riches story, vin du garage, or "garage wine" was born. Other wineries got in on the act. In 1996, Comte Stephan von Neipperg of **Chateau Canon-La-Gaffeliere** (http://www.neipperg.com/) introduced a garage wine called **La Mondotte**. **Chateau Teyssier** produces Le Dome and Chateau La Forge. The rarity of the wine makes it an attractive investment for wine lovers but some experts question the sustainability of this new style of wine making.

Pomerol

Pomerol is a small appellation that is centred around the village of Pomerol. Most of its estates are fairly small but in the 20th century a few of them, notably Petrus, Chateau LePin and Chateau LaFleur gained huge status among wine collectors. It is believed that the area was first used to grow vines in Roman times. During the Middle Ages, there was a Priory associated with the Knights Hospitallers of Saint John of Jerusalem in the area. They made their wine for the benefit of passing pilgrims. A few estates still have marker stones engraved with their emblems.

One of the world's most expensive wines can be found in the Pomerol appellation. **Pétrus** is prized for its rarity as well as its outstanding quality.

While the tiny estate dates back to the 18th century, its legend really began under the curatorship of Madame Loubat and Jean-Pierre Moueix. It became popular in the 1960s in the United States after John F Kennedy spoke highly of it. A stellar rating by wine expert Robert Parker further added to its prestige.

Pétrus is produced from Merlot grapes and is grown on a unique plateau of blue clay that is 40 million years old. The estate utilizes vines of up to 70 years old and has initiated its own cloning program. It produces only 2,500 cases annually and these sell at prices comparable with First Growth wines on the Left Bank. Pétrus is currently owned and managed by the Moueix family.

Château Lafleur and Château Le Gay once formed part of a greater property Le Manoir de Gay. From the 1940s, both estates were run by the Robin sisters. When Marie Robin died, Jacques Guinaudeau took over **Château Lafleur**, but was forced to sell its sibling property, Château Le Gay. Along with Pétrus, Château Lafleur is regarded as one of Pomerol's finest vintages, described as silky, rich and concentrated. It is best approached after 20 to 30 years of aging and a truly great vintage can still be enjoyed at 50 years. The wines are blended from Merlot and Cabernet Franc.

Château Le Gay
(http://www.vignoblespereverge.com/en/vin/chateau-le-gay-pomerol/) was acquired by Catherine Pere-Verge.
Chateau La Fleur Petrus is located on the same plateau near Petrus and Chateau La Fleur. It is owned and managed by the same family as Petrus. The estate grows 90 percent Merlot and 10 percent Cabernet Franc and its wines are smooth and concentrated but less intense than Petrus.

Château Hosanna (http://www.moueix.com/) lies adjacent to Petrus and Château Lafleur. Originally named Château Certan-Giraud, it was renamed when Christian Moueix acquired the property in 1999. The wines of Château Hosanna are rich, elegant and concentrated. Another highly regarded winery controlled by the Moueix family is **Chateau Trotanoy**. The estate belonged to the Giraud family for almost two centuries.

Château Le Pin is one of the most expensive red wines in the world. The winery was created in 1979, when Belgian winemaker Jacques Thienpont purchased a single hectare of land and turned it into a micro-winery that produced less than 750 cases of wine per year. After an enthusiastic rating from Robert Parker for the 1982 vintage, the demand rose steeply. Small parcels of land were subsequently added. The property grows 93 percent Merlot and 7 percent Cabernet Franc. Its wines are lush and concentrated, approachable at a young age but best after 7 to 10 years of aging. Château Le Pin is regarded by some as the "grandfather" of garage wines.

The largest three properties in the Pomerol appellation are Château Nénin, **Château de Sales** and Château LaPointe. Chateau de Sales (http://www.chateau-de-sales.com/welcome.html) has belonged to the same family for more than five and a half centuries. At 48 hectares, it is also the largest estate in Pomerol. It was acquired by Bertrand de Sauvanelles in 1464 but only became a winery towards the end of the 1700s. Wines produced are both light and rustic with prominent aromas of red fruit.

Château Nénin (http://www.domaines-delon.com/en/nenin-chateau_nenin_vins.html) is one of the larger wineries in the Pomerol appellation at 35 hectares. Its terroir comprises gravel-sand to gravel clay with traces of iron.

The vineyards can be traced back to the Despujol family in the mid-19th century and the château is now owned by Jean Hubert Delon and his sister Genevieve. Under their management, additional land has been acquired from neighbouring properties.

Château Nénin presently grows 78 percent Merlot, 21 percent Cabernet Franc and 1 percent Cabernet Sauvignon. Traditional methods are used and the wine is aged in casks of new oak. Its primary wine is Nénin, an elegant, powerful wine that ages well and pairs with classical meat dishes, game, roasted chicken and Asian cuisine. It is at its best at about 30 years and certain vintages can still be enjoyed at 50 years. A second wine, Fugue de Nénin is smooth, silky and ready for consumption at a slightly earlier age.

Château La Pointe (http://www.chateaulapointe.com/) dates from 1845 when it was owned by the Chaperon family and who built its beautiful chateau. In 1868, the publication *Charles Cocks' Bordeaux et ses vins* described its vines as one of Pomerol's finest growths. Today, the wines are considered great value for money. At 23 hectares, it is the third largest winery in Pomerol.

Château Beauregard (http://www.chateau-beauregard.com/) is one of the older properties in Pomerol. It was founded by Bernard Beauregard in the 17th century and began to grow vines a century later. Its delightful chateau was designed by Victor Leon who is also responsible for the Grand Theater in the city of Bordeaux. It grows a higher proportion of Cabernet Franc grapes than most estates in the appellation and produces an elegant wine that is rich in tannin.

Chateau Clinet (http://www.chateauclinet.com/) is located on the Pomerol Plateau. The cultivation of wine began here in the 17th century with the de Gombault family but its image was transformed when Jean-Michel Arcaute took over in the 1980s and introduced various reforms. The estate grows 85 percent Merlot, 10 percent Cabernet Franc and 5 percent Cabernet Sauvignon. In one parcel, known as "La Grand Vigne", it has some of the oldest vines in Pomerol, some dating back to 1934. Horses are used for ploughing and grapes are picked by hand. The wine is aged in casks of French oak. Although this smooth wine is approachable at an early age it improves after 10 years. The 1989 and 2009 vintages scored 100 points, according to *Wine Spectator's* Robert Parker. The chateau is now operated by Ronan Laborde. A tour of the vineyards and cellars can be arranged by appointment on weekdays.

Lalande de Pomerol

Lalande de Pomerol is located to the north of Pomerol. It consists of two villages, Lalande-de-Pomerol and Néac and the terroir around Néac - with its deep clay and gravel - is particularly beneficial for growing the merlot grape. There are a number of wineries worth investigating.

Château Tournefeuille (http://www.chateau-tournefeuille.com/en) is located just across the Barbanne River from Petrus. The estate has produced wine for over 200 years and its wines were awarded a gold medal at the Concours Mondial des Vins de Bordeaux in Bordeaux. It offers visitors tours and tastings and can also be booked as guest accommodation.

Other notable estates include Chateau La Fleur de Bouard (http://www.lafleurdebouard.com/en/chateau_la_fleur_de_bouard.html), Chateau de Chambrun, Chateau Les Cruzelles and Château Bertineau St Vincent, until recently owned by the family of renowned wine consultant, Michel Rolland.

Fronsac & Canon-Fronsac

Some believe that Fronsac was the original birthplace of Bordeaux wine. Tetra de Fronsac was once the site of a Gaulish oppidum (an ancient fortified town) and still retains signs of Roman settlement in the ruins of villas and temples.

Charlemagne built a fort here, loved the area's wines and is reputed to have suggested several modifications to the winemaking process, including the use of wooden barrels.

Cardinal Richelieu was another influential figure in the history of Fronsac wines. He owned a chateau in the area that makes wine to this day.

Before the 19th century, Fronsac was one of the most popular wine regions and wine from Canon-Fronsac was the first to be auctioned at Christies of London. Today, visitors can enjoy a picturesque countryside of rolling hills. The area's microclimate protects the vines from frost which is particularly beneficial for growing Merlot and Malbec.

Vintages from Canon-Fronsac are ruby red in color, with a purplish tinge and carry aromas of red and black fruit like strawberries, raspberries, red currant and prunes.

There are two main villages in Canon-Fronsac: Saint Michel de Fronsac and Fronsac. Other communes that are included in the Fronsac (but not Canon-Fronsac) appellation include La Riviere, Saint Germain de la Riviere, Saint Aignan, Saillans and Galgon.

At Chateau La Croix in Fronsac on the Right Bank, visitors can combine wine tasting with a rare French delicacy: truffles. The estate is owned by the Dorneau family and grows 70 percent Merlot, 25 percent Cabernet Franc and 5 percent Cabernet Sauvignon. It produces a charming, elegant wine. Visitors will be able to sample the suggested wine/truffle pairings. Chateau La Croix is located in the southeast of the Canon-Fronsac appellation.

Other recommended wineries include Chateau de La Dauphine (https://www.chateau-dauphine.com/?lang=en), Chateau Fontenil, Chateau Villars and Chateau Vrai Canon Bouche.

Côtes de Bourg & Côtes de Bordeaux

Côtes de Bourg is one of the oldest appellations in Bordeaux dating from Roman times when its strategic location led to the early settlement and fortification of the area. The region has a number of interesting archaeological sites which attest to its roots.

Recommended wineries in the area include Roc de Cambes (http://www.roc-de-cambes.com/), Chateau Bone (http://www.chateaubone.com/), Clos de Moiselles, Chateau Mercier (http://www.chateau-mercier.fr/GB/index.html) and Fougas Maldoror.

In 2009 Côtes de Bourg resisted inclusion in the new super-appellation of Côtes de Bordeaux. Côtes de Bordeaux includes Côtes de Blaye, Côtes de Castillon and Côtes de Francs

Côtes de Blaye is located to the north of Côtes de Bourg and its wines also date to Roman times. It represents 40 communes and over 400 wineries. The main grape varieties are Merlot, Cabernet Sauvignon and Malbec and you will also find less common white varieties such as Colombard and Ugni Blanc. Its top quality produce can qualify for labeling as Premieres Côtes de Blaye.

Recommended wineries include Chateau la Croix de Perenne (which belonged to Saint Romaine de Blaye abbey until the French Revolution) and Chateau Marechaux, Chateau Belle Colline and Chateau Gigault (all three the property of wine negociant Christophe Reboul. Also of interest is Dominique Leandre Chevalier, which produces Trecolore, one of the few vintages in Bordeaux made from 100 percent Petit Verdot.

Côtes de Castillon was named after Castillon la Bataille, one of the decisive battlesites of the Hundred Year War. It lies east of St Emilion and south of Fronsac. The appellation includes nine communes and around 350 wineries of which a third are involved in local cooperatives.

Its main grape types are Merlot and Cabernet Franc and its wines are similar in character and quality as those from St Emilion. Recommended wineries include Chateau d'Aiguilhe, Chateau Clos L'Eglise, Chateau Cap de Faugeres (http://www.chateau-cap-de-faugeres.com/), Clos Lunelles (http://www.vignoblesperse.com/en/vin/5/clos-lunelles) and Chateau Joanin Becot.

Côtes de Francs is the smallest of the appellations included in Côtes de Bordeaux and lies east of St Emilion. It consists of only 490 hectares and has less than 50 wineries. Best known of these is the Chateau Le Puy (http://www.chateau-le-puy.com/en/) which has been owned by the Amoreau family for more than 400 years.

Entre Deux Mers

Entre Deux Mers is located between the Dordogne and Garonne River and the appellation is known for its fruity white wines that can approached at a relatively young age. At 10,000 hectares, it is one of the largest appellations and its history dates from Roman times.

The Appellation of Cotes de Bourdeaux falls within the territory of Entre Deux Mers and the region also includes Sainte Croix du Mont, Sainte Macaire, Graves de Vayres, Sainte Foy Bordeaux, Loupiac and Cadillac.

Loupiac, Cadellac and Sainte-Croix-du-Mont are known for their sweet white wines that can be regarded as Right Bank alternatives to those from Sauternes. **Clos Jean** in Loupiac, **Château Manos** in Cadellac, and Château du Pavillon and **Château la Rame** (http://www.chateaularame.com/en/our-wines.aspx) in Sainte-Croix-du-Mont are good examples.

Red wines from this area may use the labelling Bordeaux or Bordeaux Superieur. **Chateau Reignac** (https://reignac.com/en/) offers visitors the opportunity of strolling through their scent garden, tasting the fabulous reds in a 15th century pigeon house or viewing a greenhouse designed by Gustave Eiffel.

Other examples of red wines from this area are **Château Marjosse** (http://www.chateau-marjosse.fr/), which is run by Pierre Lurton - owner of Chateau Cheval Blanc in St Emilion, **Chateau Gree Laroque**, **Chateau Hostens Picant** (http://chateauhostens-picant.fr/en/), **Chateau Pey La Tour**, **Domaine de Courteillac** (http://domainedecourteillac.com/domaine-courteillac-uk/) and **Chateau Carignan** (http://www.chateau-carignan.fr/?ln=en) which dates back to the 1400s

Chateau Thieley (http://thieuley.com/en/) produces both red and white wines. The winery is open for visits and tastings and also offers guest accommodation.

Chateau Rauzan Despagne (http://despagne.fr/), which produces both red and white wine, was originally a hunting lodge in the 17th century.

Buying Wine from Bordeaux

The Bordeaux wine trade has a business model that was established several centuries ago. Many chateaux do not offer wine sales directly. The bulk of the wine is sold through brokers (known as courtiers) to a class of merchants known as negociants. They in turn make the wine available to countries across the globe. This system has been in place for hundreds of years and goes by the name of La Place de Bordeaux.

A significant portion of the wine is sold as futures, or en primeur meaning that it is sold prior to bottling and while still in the barrel.

Before the 20th century bottling was outsourced to the negociants. The first chateau that began to bottle its wine on site was Chateau Mouton Rothschild and by the mid-20th century, many chateaux had made the shift. In 1969 St Emilion made it a legal requirement that all of its estates had to bottle their own wines.

Where to Buy

For the general public, there are several options for buying wine. You can get great deals on bulk buys directly from the estate only if they are open to the public and offer onsite sales. Wine merchants, on the other hand, will be able to introduce you to a large and diverse range of wines. Here you can often taste the wine before purchasing.

What to Buy

You should carefully assess which wines present value for money. Here are several pointers that may be helpful. The website Wine Cellar Insider (http://www.thewinecellarinsider.com/) publishes a vintage chart which scores the growing season of each year from 1959 to the present and also provides details about harvest conditions and tasting notes. A great vintage is defined as a year in which excellent wines resulted from all appellations and across a wide spectrum of classes.

An influential 100-point scale for rating wine was invented by Robert Parker. The London International Vintner's Exchange was founded in 1999 as a sales platform for investment grade wine. Like a stock exchange, it offers several indexes that track the ever-shifting value of its wine listings.

Budget Buying Tips

If you love powerful intense wines, but do not have the budget for a Pauillac try a St Julien. Wines from this neighbouring appellation are often similar in character.

If you like sweet wines but cannot afford Sauternes look at the wines from Loupiac, Cadellac and Sainte-Croix-du-Mont which can be purchased for a fraction of the price.

There are several ways to buy a bottle of interesting wine from Bordeaux without breaking the bank. Explore the Bourgeois Cru classification, which ranks just below the Cru Classe wines or buy a Second Wine from one of the classed estates. Explore appellations that can be found adjacent or concurrent to the top-ranking terroirs, such as Graves, Medoc, Haut-Medoc, Fronsac, Lalande-de-Pomerol, Montagne-St-Émilion and Côtes de Castillon.

If you are in France during autumn keep your eyes open for the annual Wine Fair. From September to October, various French supermarket chains such as Carrefour, Auchan and E. Leclerc participate in the promotion, enabling their customers to buy good Bordeaux wines at reasonable prices.

There are several online websites that buy and sell Bordeaux wines. If you are unsure about the price, compare vintages and brands on the site Wine Searcher (http://www.winesearcher.com).

If you are in the USA, great way to connect with other lovers of Bordeaux wine is by joining the Commanderie de Bordeaux (http://www.commanderie.org/), an organization with chapters in various cities with links to other wine organizations.

Beware of counterfeit wines. Buy your vintages from reputable sources and pay special attention to great vintage years and any wines bottled prior to 1980 as these are more likely to be fake. Some wineries have begun to use laser-engraved labels and in 2015, St Emilion became the first appellation to introduce their own barcoding system.

Wine Tourism

Bordeaux offers wine lovers a variety of tours, workshops and unique experiences. You can learn more about specialized food-wine pairings, attend harvesting workshops, pruning workshops, wine blending workshops or even stay in a chateau and soak up the local flavor for a truly immersive experience.

There are wines to suit every taste and trend. Various tour companies will be able to tailor a wine tasting holiday to your liking or you can construct your own itinerary around personal preferences.

If you want to visit one of the top estates you should contact them well in advance. Certain estates limit accessibility to just wine industry professionals. Most wine estates allow the public to visit by appointment only and few are open on Saturdays or Sundays. Alternatively, if you are already in Bordeaux, local wine merchants will probably be able to connect you with a wine estate or two. Do not forget to factor in travel time between estates and wine regions. Realistically, you will probably be able to visit about 3 estates per day.

Do not forget to spend some time in the lovely city of Bordeaux. There are several sites of interest to wine lovers. La Cite du Vin (http://www.laciteduvin.com/en/) offers an interactive experience that factors in various aspects and themes around the world of wine and includes a glass of wine. Visit the Musee du Vin et du Negoce (http://www.museeduvinbordeaux.com/), if you wish to learn more about the fascinating history of Bordeaux wines. The experience includes a tasting workshop.

There are several wine apps will be complimentary to a Bordeaux trip. Use the Bordeaux Wine Trip app to navigate your way to the region's best vineyards, wine bars, restaurants and other attractions. With the Smart Bordeaux app, you will have detailed information to wines, winemakers, terroirs and other facts. It could be worth your while to download the Bernard Magrez app, which has information about the produce of various Bordeaux wineries owned and controlled by Magrez.

Pauillac Tourist Office
La Verrerie, 33250 Pauillac, France
Tel: +33 5 56 59 03 08

St Emilion Tourist Office
Place des Créneaux, 33330 Saint-Émilion, France
Tel: +33 5 57 55 28 28

Pomerol Oenotourism
38 Route de Nouet, 33910 Saint-Denis-de-Pile, France
Tel: +33 6 69 41 19 29

Staying at a Winery

Margaux

Château Giscours
http://www.chateau-giscours.fr/
Guest accommodation in the 19th century chateau.

Chateau du Tertre
http://chateaudutertre.fr/en/home/
Guest accommodation.

Saint Estephe

Château Ormes de Pez
Accommodation in 18th century chateau.

Graves

Château Pape Clément
http://www.bernard-magrez.com/en/wines/chateau-pape-clement
Guest accommodation, TV, private bathroom and free Wi-Fi.

St Emilion

Chateau Valandraud
http://www.thunevin.com/chateau-valandraud
Five rooms available, free tasting included for guests.

Château Franc Grâce-Dieu
http://www.chateaufrancgracedieu.com/en/
Five rooms available.

Château Troplong Mondot
http://www.chateau-troplong-mondot.com/
Accommodation in several individually decorated rooms.

Côtes de Bourg

Chateau Mercier
http://www.chateau-mercier.fr/GB/gite/heberg00.html
Various sizes of rooms available.

Entre-deux-Mers

Chateau Thieley
http://thieuley.com/en/
Bed & breakfast. Two rooms available.

Winery Tours & Workshops

Pauillac

Château Lafite Rothschild
http://www.lafite.com/en/
Tour with tasting. Private tours on weekday afternoons at 2pm or 3.30pm. By appointment only.

Château Pichon Longueville Baron
http://www.pichonbaron.com/en/
Guided tour and tastings by appointment

Château Duhart-Milon
http://www.lafite.com/en/the-chateaus/chateau-duhart-milon/
Tour with tasting. By appointment only. Closed from August to October.

Château Pontet-Canet
http://www.pontet-canet.com/en/
Tour of vineyards, vat room and cellar, followed by a wine tasting.

Château Lynch-Bages
http://www.jmcazes.com/en/chateau-lynch-bages/
60 minute tour followed by tasting of 2 wines. This is one of only a handful of wineries that are open by appointment on Saturdays and Sundays. Free art exhibition of a contemporary artist from May to October. There is also a bakery, brasserie and gift shop.

Margaux

Château Brane-Cantenac
(http://www.brane-cantenac.com/en/)
Guided walk, gourmet tastings with cheese and wine.

Château Desmirail
(http://www.desmirail.com/)
Tours and tastings

Château Kirwan
(http://www.chateau-kirwan.com/)
Guided tours, tastings, lunch and dinner.

Château Giscours
http://www.chateau-giscours.fr/
Guided tours, tastings and wine workshops.

Chateau Marquis d'Alesme
https://www.marquisdalesme.wine/en/home
Guided tours and tastings, plus a child-friendly introduction to wine-making.

Chateau du Tertre
http://chateaudutertre.fr/en/home/
Tours and tastings. By appointment.

Chateau Dauzac
http://www.chateaudauzac.com/
Visits, guided tours and tastings. Historical buildings, an arboretum of rare trees and the honey produced on-site is available to the public.

St Julien

Château Léoville-Poyferré
http://www.leoville-poyferre.fr/en/
Basic tour & tasting by appointment: buy wines and souvenirs from the gift shop

Château Lagrange
http://chateau-lagrange.com/en/
Offers tours, tastings and group dining opportunities upon request. Also available for hosting events.

Saint Estephe

Château Lafon-Rochet
http://www.lafon-rochet.com/
Visit and tasting by appointment.

Château Phélan Ségur
http://www.phelansegur.com/
Visit and tasting by appointment.

Haut-Medoc

Château La Tour Carnet
http://www.bernard-magrez.com/en/wines/chateau-la-tour-carnet-0
Visits by appointment.

Pessac-Leognan

Château Pape Clément
http://www.bernard-magrez.com/en/wines/chateau-pape-clement
Visits and tastings. Property includes a chapel and a gift shop. By appointment.

Chateau Smith Haut Lafitte
http://www.smith-haut-lafitte.com/en/smith-haut-lafitte-visite.html
Basic tastings, plus a variety of themed experiences, including food/wine pairings with chocolate and dried fruit as well as a wine-making workshop and an art and wine tour.

Chateau Carbonnieux
http://carbonnieux.com/?lang=en
Visits by appointment. The estate has a boutique shop that sells wine, souvenirs, honey, grape jelly and books. There is also a permanent exhibition of antique cars, jugs and wine making tools on site.

Château Bouscaut
http://www.chateau-bouscaut.com/uk
Cheese and wine tastings, food and wine pairings, workshop that guides visitors in the art of blending their own wines

Sauternes

Château d'Yquem
http://yquem.fr/int-en/
Guided tour and tasting by appointment.

Château Guiraud
http://chateauguiraud.fr/en/
Guided tour. Booking via the website.

Château La Tour Blanche
http://www.tour-blanche.com/
Guided tours and gourmet visits. Special lunch with food/wine pairings.

Chateau Suduiraut
http://www.suduiraut.com/en/
Private tours, an aroma workshop and a tasting menu.

Château Filhot
http://www.filhot.com/chateau-filhot-sauternes-second-growth-classified-in-1855-4001.dhtml
Guided visits by appointment.

Château d'Arche
http://chateau-arche.com/
Audio guided tour of the vineyards.

Chateau Clos Haut Peyraguey
http://www.bernard-magrez.com/en/wines/chateau-clos-haut-peyraguey
Visits and wine tasting.

Château Rabaud-Promis
http://rabaud-promis.com/z/site.php?act=4
Visits and tastings by appointment.

Chateau de Rayne Vigneau
http://www.raynevigneau.fr/en/
Visits and tastings, horseback rides through the vineyards.

Château Rieussec
http://www.lafite.com/en/the-chateaus/chateau-rieussec/
Tasting and tour. Mondays, Thursdays and Fridays. Closed from August to November. By appointment only.

Cerrons

Chateau de Cerons
http://www.chateaudecerons.com/the-wines/
Tour & tasting.

St Emilion

Château Pavie
http://www.vignoblesperse.com/en/
Hour-long tour and tasting. By appointment.

Château Fombrauge
http://www.bernard-magrez.com/en/wines/chateau-fombrauge
Visits by appointment.

Chateau Beau-Sejour Becot
http://www.beausejour-becot.com/
Visits and tastings by appointment.

Chateau La Dominique
http://en.chateau-ladominique.com/
Besides several tailored tour and tasting experiences, you can also learn to train your tongue with guided tastings or a tasting workshop. Food and wine tasting opportunities also exist. There is a shop that sells wine, books and lifestyle accessories.

Pomerol

Château L'Évangile
http://www.lafite.com/en/the-chateaus/chateau-levangile/
Tour and tasting. Tours only on Tuesdays and Wednesdays at specific times. Closed from August to October.

Chateau Clinet
http://www.chateauclinet.com/
Tour of the vineyard and cellars by appointment.

Fronsac

Chateau La Dauphine
https://www.chateau-dauphine.com/oenotourisme/
Tour & tasting.

Côtes de Castillon

Chateau Cap de Faugeres
http://www.chateau-cap-de-faugeres.com/
Tour and Tastings. Facilities for visitors with reduced mobility available.

Entre deux Mers

Chateau de Reignac
https://reignac.com/en/
Tour & tasting. Unique features include a scent garden and a 15th century pigeon house. Winner of Wine Tourism award (2015)

Chateau Carignan
http://www.chateau-carignan.fr/
Visit and tasting by appointment.

Chateau Thieley
http://thieuley.com/en/
Visit and tastings.

Chateau La Rame
http://www.chateaularame.com/en/
Tour & tasting

Glossary

AOC or Appellation d'origine controlee: A term used to describe a French system that designates geographical indications for agricultural products such as wine, spirits, cheese, butter, honey, lavender and other items.

Aroma: A wine's fragrance

Botrytized Wine: Wine that was produced from grapes infected with the *Botrytis cinerea* fungus, also known as noble rot.

Claret: A red wine from the Bordeaux region.

Cryoextraction: A process that involves freezing the grapes before they are pressed to reduce the amount of water in the juice.

Cuvee: The term can refer to a blend of wine from different grape types or to wine from specially designated barrels or vats. Although it can also be used to indicate quality, it is not connected to any particular system of classification.

Decanting: The process of pouring wine from one vessel to another. In older wines, this is done to separate the sediment from the wine, but the process can also release the aroma of a younger wine.

Decanter: A vessel into which wine is decanted.

Dessert Wine: A sweet wine that accompanies dessert or is immediately preceded by dessert

Drinking Window: The period during which a particular wine can be drunk with the optimum amount of pleasure.

Dry: The opposite of sweet. Dry wines have no residual sugars.

En primeur: En primeur refers to the trade in wine futures. This means that the wine is purchased (usually by negociants) at an early stage of development, while still in the barrel and prior to being bottled. The advantage of this strategy is usually to obtain a good wine at a slightly cheaper rate, although the appreciation of a particular vintage may include some risk. In the case of wines of limited production, it is often the only way to obtain a few bottles. Typically, the wine is sampled when it is about 6-8 months old. It is then given a preliminary rating based on expected quality. It is usually paid a year or even 18 months prior to the official release.

Fermentation: The process that converts various types of sugars into alcohol.

Flavor Intensity: This describes how strong or weak a wine's taste is.

Fruit Forward: A term used to describe a wine which has a prominent flavour of fruitiness.

Full-bodied: A term that describes a wine with a fairly high tannin and alcohol content. In other words, a wine that tends to overpower the palate with its texture and intensity.

Glycerol: A component of the wine that plays a huge role in its mouth-feel, in other words, it lends weight and smoothness to the wine without adding sugars or alcohol.

Hectoliters: A unit used to measure volume equal to 100 liters. It is often used for wine, beer and agricultural produce.

Jerobeam: A wine bottle with a capacity four times the size of a normal 750ml wine bottle.

Malolactic fermentation: A secondary fermentation process that converts the malic acid present in grapes to lactic acid, which is softer on the palate.

Negociant: A wine merchant that buys grapes or wine in various stages of development and then sells and ships the bottled wine as a wholesaler.

Noble Rot: Noble rot occurs when moist conditions in the vineyard cause infection by a beneficial grey fungus known as *Botrytis cinerea*. When infection is followed by a dry cycle, the grape raisins, a process which concentrates its sugar content. The resulting harvest produces a sweet wine that is also known as botrytized wine.

Nose: How the smell of the wine expresses itself. This is a combination of its aroma and bouquet.

Oenologist: An expert in the field of wine making.

Oenology: The study of wines

Oenophile: Wine lover

Phenolic Maturity: Ripeness; when the skin, seed and pulp of the grape has ripened.

Polyphenols: A type of compound found mainly in the skin, but also in the berry of the grape. Polyphenols contribute to the color and tannin level of the wine.

Residual Sugar: The amount of sugar that remains in a wine after fermentation

Sommelier: A wine waiter

Table Wine: Any wine with an alcohol content between 7 and 14 percent that is not sparkling or fortified. In the EU, this could also refer to a wine of lower quality.

Tannin: Tannin refers to the occurrence of certain molecules in a wine that enhances its texture, full-bodied taste and aging potential. It derives from skins and seeds as well as wood particles present in the barrel. When present, tannin leaves a dry taste in the mouth.

Terroir: A French term that describes the influence of factors such as land, soil type, climate and environment on wines.

Veraison: This term refers to the stage in grape growth when the berries transform from small, hard, acidic berries, to the softer, sweeter ones that characterize ripening grapes.

Vigneron: A person who cultivates grapes for wine-making

Vintage: The harvest year for the grapes used to produce that particular wine.

Vine Density: The number of vines planted per hectare. This varies and can also play a role in the character of a wine.

Viticulture: Either the cultivation of grapes or a study of the cultivation of grapes

93038401R00055

Made in the USA
Columbia, SC
03 April 2018